Mr. Food
TEST KITCHEN

Sinful Sweets &
TASTY TREATS

More Than 150 Desserts Sure to Satisfy Your Sweet Tooth

Best-Selling Author with Millions of Cookbooks Sold

Inquiries should be addressed to:
Cogin, Inc.
1770 NW 64 Street, Suite 500
Fort Lauderdale, FL 33309

Book design concept: Rachel Johnson
Design & layout: Grand Design/Lorraine Dan
Photography: Kelly Rusin

Library of Congress Cataloging-in-Publication Data
Mr. Food Test Kitchen
Mr. Food Test Kitchen Sinful Sweets & Tasty Treats/ Mr. Food Test Kitchen

ISBN 978-0-9755396-4-4

Cookery. 2. Quick and Easy. I. Title: Mr. Food Test Kitchen Sinful Sweets & Tasty Treats. II. Title.
Printed in the United States of America
First Edition
www.MrFood.com

Introduction

Let's admit it...if we could, we'd all eat dessert first!

That's exactly why your mouth is probably watering just looking at all the awesome desserts awaiting you. Every chapter in this cookbook is brimming with the easiest and tastiest desserts you could dream of!

And if you think avoiding temptation is difficult as you flip through this book, just imagine what it was like working in our offices adjacent to our Test Kitchen...or in the Test Kitchen itself as every single recipe was tested, tasted and tested again and again. Yes, at least three times, to make sure each one met our standards and yours! That triple-tested guarantee is what sets this book apart from most other cookbooks. It assures you that if we could make the recipe better and easier, we did. That means you get only foolproof recipes you can make time and time again with confidence.

This collection of more than 150 quick and easy recipes will taste like you have a pastry chef hidden in your kitchen; but you'll get to take all of the credit! We know you can hardly wait to begin; especially if you've taken a peek at what's in store. Yes, loads of new recipes; plus we've included a few of our very best TV recipes that have earned rave reviews.

And besides having each member of the Test Kitchen feature some of their personal favorites, they also include lots of handy Test Kitchen Tips to help guide you along the way.

So, get your "just desserts" by making and serving these sinful sweets and tasty treats. Like our creamy homemade shortcut version of Toasted Coconut Cream Pie, it'll do you proud. Get ready to be on the receiving end of raves when you place our Chocolate Sandwich Cookie Cake on the table next time company comes calling. Picture the look of delight on your kids or grandkids faces when you offer them some homemade Confetti Chocolate Bars when they ask for a snack. Dazzle everyone during the holiday season with our eye-catching holiday specialties like Dutch Apple Crumb Pie and Pumpkin Spice Roll. There's something here for every sweet indulgence, every heavenly craving, and every occasion.

And if you can't help yourself, and find that you have chosen to eat dessert first; that means you have a pure zest for living life to the fullest, just like us. And with these recipes, you'll be on your way; to endless "OOH IT'S SO GOOD!!®"

Pictured on front cover (l-r): Patty Rosenthal -Test Kitchen Director, Howard Rosenthal - Chief Food Officer, Art Ginsburg - aka Mr. Food, Kelly Rusin - Food Stylist/Photographer.

Acknowledgements

With an entire team that loves desserts, we had a lot of enthusiasm for working on this cookbook! In fact, most days we were very thankful to all of our viewers and readers for asking us to create a desserts only cookbook! So THANK YOU first to everyone who encouraged us to work on this collection of to-die-for dessert recipes. Your requests made coming to work a very sweet experience every single day.

We're indebted to Howard Rosenthal, whose leadership, boundless energy, exceptional expertise in the kitchen and creative vision is at the heart of every single production and project that comes from the Mr. Food brand. His seal of approval means you can count on the "best of the best" from all of us.

Our equally hardworking Test Kitchen Supervisor, Patty Rosenthal is the perfect complement to this dynamic duo. She may be known as our resident "chocoholic," but when it comes to all of the sweet recipes in this book, her sharp eye for detail ensures that you will be able to recreate these recipes easily at home. She is amazing, and truly has the gift of "good taste!"

And of course, there is no "I" in team so we want to tip our chef hats at Jaime Gross and the rest of the Test Kitchen team for helping us test, taste and retest every recipe over and over until they were just right. And since we also eat with our eyes, thanks need to go to Kelly Rusin for the creativity and sunshine she brings to the kitchen and studio through her creativity and photography. To Hal Silverman, for his expertise and attention to detail, for his preproduction skills and making us want to dig into each photo. And as you can imagine, all that baking can get pretty messy at times, so thanks to Dave DiCarlo for always keeping our Test Kitchen looking spic and span.

As our Test Kitchen finished developing or updating each recipe, it was our busy publishing division that continued the process of perfecting this cookbook. We are indebted once again to Jodi Flayman, who worked tirelessly to coordinate, document and verify every detail of every recipe, photo, and fact that you will find in this book. We couldn't manage without her. We are grateful to Helayne Rosenblum for bringing many parts of this book to life with her engaging way with words. Many thanks to Carol Ginsburg for her skillful eye when it comes to proofreading, ensuring that all the recipes in this book meet our strict criteria for being easy-to-read and accurate. And to Rachel Johnson, thanks for your easy-to-read page design.

Behind the scenes, Steve Ginsburg keeps every division of our entire company running flawlessly; plus he was always willing to taste every single dessert recipe we were testing – even if it was right after breakfast! He is a trooper! And to Ethel Ginsburg, aka "Mrs. Food", thanks for sharing our passion for all things sweet.

Also, special thanks go to Lorraine Dan for her artful design and layout of this mouthwatering collection along with the entire production team who helps make putting a book like this together seem so easy. Thank you!

Last but not least, once again, it is our founder, Art Ginsburg who you all know and love as Mr. Food, who continues to inspire each and every one of us to do our very best, in the tradition that he began. Thank you doesn't even seem enough for all he has done to make being part of the Mr. Food team such an amazing and sweet experience. Every day that we work together with him, is a day we are all thankful for...and one that begins and ends with **"OOH IT'S SO GOOD!! ®"**

Contents

Dedicated to:

Everyone who has stress in their lives....and isn't that most of us?

Did you know that *DESSERTS* is *STRESSED* spelled backwards?

So, we hope you use these recipes to make your life a bit sweeter.

Cakes & Cupcakes

Chocolate Sandwich Cookie Cake

Serves 16

- 1 (18.25-ounce) package devil's food cake mix
- 1 (8-ounce) package cream cheese, softened
- ½ cup sugar
- 2 cups frozen whipped topping, thawed
- 12 chocolate sandwich cookies, coarsely crushed
- 1 (16-ounce) container chocolate fudge frosting

1 Preheat oven to 350 degrees F. Prepare cake mix according to package directions for 2 (9-inch) round cake pans. Bake according to package directions; let cool 15 minutes.

2 In a large bowl, beat cream cheese and sugar with an electric mixer until blended. Gently stir in whipped topping and crushed cookies.

3 Place 1 cake layer on wire rack and spread with cream cheese mixture. Top with remaining cake layer. Let stand 10 minutes, or until firm.

4 Spoon frosting into a microwaveable bowl; microwave until melted, 45 to 60 seconds, stirring frequently. Starting in center of cake, pour frosting over cake and let drizzle down sides. Refrigerate 30 minutes, or until ready to serve.

About this Recipe:

When we first tasted this in our Test Kitchen, everyone gave Patty, our Test Kitchen Director, a double thumbs up. After that, our whole team asked if they could have the recipe...before it even went to print.

Strawberry Shortcake Torte

Serves 10

1 (18.25-ounce) package yellow cake mix, batter prepared according to package directions

3 pints fresh strawberries, hulled

2 cups (1 pint) heavy cream

1 tablespoon confectioners' sugar

1 teaspoon vanilla extract

1 Bake cake batter according to package directions for 2 (9-inch) round layers; let cool. Slice each cake layer in half horizontally, making 4 layers, and place 1 layer on a serving platter.

2 Slice 2 pints of strawberries and set aside.

3 In a large bowl with an electric mixer on high speed, beat heavy cream, sugar, and vanilla until stiff peaks form. Spread one-quarter of whipped cream mixture over top of first cake layer. Top with one-third of sliced strawberries. Repeat with remaining layers, topping final layer with remaining whole strawberries, hulled-side down.

4 Cover loosely and chill at least 2 hours before serving. Keep refrigerated.

Serving Suggestion:
To make this even more summery fresh, pick up some fresh mint at the market and garnish each slice with a piece right before serving.

Chocolate Peanut Butter Cup Cake

Serves 15

- 1 (18.25-ounce) package chocolate cake mix
- 30 miniature peanut butter cup candies, coarsely chopped, reserving 3/4 cup for garnish
- 1 (8-ounce) package cream cheese, softened
- ½ cup creamy peanut butter
- ½ stick butter, softened
- 2-½ cups confectioners' sugar
- 1 tablespoon milk
- 1 teaspoon vanilla extract

1 Preheat oven to 350 degrees F. Coat a 9- x 13-inch baking dish with cooking spray.

2 In a large bowl, prepare batter according to package directions. Stir in peanut butter cups and pour into prepared baking dish.

3 Bake 30 to 35 minutes, or until a toothpick inserted in center comes out clean. Cool completely in pan on a wire rack.

4 Meanwhile, in a large bowl with an electric mixer on medium speed, beat cream cheese, peanut butter, and butter until creamy. Gradually add confectioners' sugar, beating on low speed until smooth; add milk and stir in vanilla until well blended. Spread evenly over cake; sprinkle with remaining peanut butter cups. Cut into squares and serve immediately, or cover and chill until ready to serve.

When measuring sticky ingredients like peanut butter, spray your measuring cup with cooking spray to easily remove them when adding to your recipes.

Slow Cookin' Spoon Cake

Serves 6

- 1 (19.8-ounce) package brownie mix
- 2 large eggs
- ¼ cup vegetable oil
- 2 tablespoons water
- ½ cup walnuts, chopped
- 1 (8-ounce) package cream cheese, softened
- ½ stick butter, softened
- ½ cup sugar
- 2 large eggs
- 1 teaspoon vanilla extract
- 2 tablespoons all-purpose flour

1 In a large bowl, stir together brownie mix, eggs, oil, and water until batter is smooth. Stir in walnuts and spoon half of brownie batter into a lightly greased 3-quart slow cooker.

2 In another large bowl with an electric mixer on medium speed, beat cream cheese and butter until creamy; gradually add sugar, beating well. Add 2 eggs, 1 at a time, beating until blended. Stir in vanilla, then fold in flour. Pour cream cheese mixture over brownie batter in slow cooker. Dollop remaining brownie batter over cream cheese mixture; swirl mixture gently with a knife.

3 Cover and cook on LOW setting 5-1/2 hours, or until set. Carefully remove slow cooker insert from heat element; let stand 45 minutes before serving.

Did You know?

If you're in the mindset that your slow-cooker is just for stews and casseroles, think again. As a matter of fact, mrfood.com has loads of easy slow-cooker recipes that fit every occasion.

Peachy Poke Cake

Serves 10

- 1 (18.25-ounce) package white cake mix
- 1 (4-serving-size) package peach-flavored gelatin
- 1 cup boiling water
- 1 (12-ounce) container frozen whipped topping, thawed
- 1 (29-ounce) can sliced peaches in juice, drained, divided

1 Prepare cake mix according to package directions for 2 (9-inch) round cake pans. Bake according to package directions; let cool 15 minutes.

2 Using the handle of a wooden spoon, poke about 15 holes randomly into each cake layer.

3 In a small bowl, dissolve gelatin in boiling water. Slowly pour into holes of both cakes. Refrigerate 30 minutes.

4 Place 1 cake layer on serving platter and frost with whipped topping; layer with half the peach slices. Place second cake layer on top and frost top and sides with remaining whipped topping. Refrigerate until ready to serve, then garnish with remaining peach slices.

Did You Know?
Poke cakes first gained popularity back in the late 1960's when recipes for these types of colorful cakes appeared on the back of boxes of gelatin. The rest is tasty history!

Southern Red Velvet Cake

Serves 12

1-½ cups vegetable shortening

1-½ cups sugar

2 eggs

2-½ cups all-purpose flour

1 tablespoon unsweetened cocoa powder

1 teaspoon baking soda

1 teaspoon salt

1 cup buttermilk

1 tablespoon vanilla extract

1 teaspoon white vinegar

2 tablespoons red food color (1-ounce bottle) (see Tip)

Cream Cheese Pecan Frosting (See recipe on next page)

1 Preheat oven to 350 degrees F. Coat 3 (8-inch) round cake pans with cooking spray and lightly flour.

2 In a large bowl with an electric mixer on medium speed, beat shortening, sugar, and eggs 2 to 3 minutes, or until light and fluffy. Add flour, cocoa, baking soda, and salt and continue beating until well mixed. Gradually add buttermilk, vanilla, and vinegar, beating 2 to 3 minutes, or until thoroughly combined. With a spoon, stir in food color until thoroughly mixed. Spoon batter equally into prepared cake pans

3 Bake 30 to 35 minutes, or until a wooden toothpick inserted in center comes out clean.

4 Cool in pans on wire racks 10 minutes. Remove from pans and cool completely on wire racks. Spread frosting between layers and on top and sides of cake. Cover loosely and chill at least 2 hours before serving.

Yes, it really takes 2 tablespoons of red food color to give this cake its deep rich red hue.

Cream Cheese Pecan Frosting

Makes 3 cups

1 (8-ounce) package cream cheese, softened

1 stick butter, softened

2-½ cups confectioners' sugar

1 teaspoon vanilla extract

1 cup chopped pecans

1 In a medium bowl with an electric mixer on medium speed, beat cream cheese, butter, confectioners' sugar, and vanilla. Increase speed to high and beat 1 to 2 more minutes, or until frosting is smooth.

2 Stir in chopped pecans until thoroughly mixed. Use immediately, or cover and chill until ready to use, allowing it to soften again when needed.

In a hurry? Soften cream cheese by removing the wrapper, placing on a microwaveable dish, and microwaving 15 seconds on high. Just don't overdo it!

Triple Chocolate Indulgence

Serves 15

- 1 (18.25-ounce) package devil's food chocolate cake mix

- 1 cup dark chocolate chips

- 1 (14-ounce) can sweetened condensed milk

- 1 (8-ounce) container frozen whipped topping, thawed

- 1 (1.55-ounce) chocolate bar

1 Preheat oven to 350 degrees F. Coat a 9- x 13-inch baking dish with cooking spray.

2 In a large bowl, prepare batter according to package directions. Stir in chocolate chips and pour batter into prepared baking dish.

3 Bake 30 to 35 minutes or until a toothpick inserted in center comes out clean.

4 Let cool 10 minutes, then using the handle of a wooden spoon, poke 18 holes in top of cake. Pour sweetened condensed milk over top of cake, letting it sink into holes. Let cool completely.

5 Top cake with whipped topping, then grate chocolate bar over top. Refrigerate until ready to serve.

When garnishing with chocolate, temperature matters! If the chocolate is too cold, you'll get really small flakes. If it's too warm, it will make a mess. When it's room temperature, you should get perfect curls of chocolate.

Loaded Chocolate Chip Cake

Serves 12

- 1 (18.25-ounce) package yellow cake mix
- 1 (6-serving-size) package instant vanilla pudding and pie filling
- 4 eggs
- ½ cup vegetable oil
- 1 cup sour cream
- 2 cups mini semi-sweet chocolate chips

1 Preheat oven to 350 degrees F. Coat a Bundt pan with cooking spray.

2 In a large bowl with an electric mixer, mix cake mix and pudding mix. Add eggs, one at a time, beating after each addition. Add oil and sour cream, beating until well combined. Stir in chocolate chips. Pour into prepared pan.

3 Bake 45 to 50 minutes, or until toothpick inserted in center comes out clean.

Team Member Favorite:

Jodi, our Project Coordinator and a huge dessert lover, always gets rave reviews every time she makes this to-die-for cake for family and friends. Now she's paying it forward, by sharing it with all of us!

Black Forest Cake Roll

Serves 10

¾ cup all-purpose flour

¼ cup unsweetened cocoa powder

1 teaspoon baking powder

¼ teaspoon salt

3 eggs

1 cup granulated sugar

⅓ cup water

1 teaspoon vanilla extract

Confectioners' sugar for sprinkling

1 (21-ounce) can cherry pie filling

2 cups thawed frozen whipped topping

Chocolate chips for sprinkling

1 Preheat oven to 375 degrees F. Line a 10- x 15-inch rimmed baking sheet with aluminum foil and coat with cooking spray.

2 In a small bowl, combine flour, cocoa, baking powder, and salt; set aside.

3 In a large bowl with an electric mixer on high speed, beat eggs and sugar. Gradually beat in water and vanilla until well blended. Reduce speed to low and beat in flour mixture just until smooth. Pour onto baking sheet. Bake 10 to 12 minutes, or until a wooden toothpick inserted in center comes out clean.

4 Sprinkle a clean kitchen towel with confectioners' sugar and invert cake onto towel. While still hot, peel off aluminum foil and roll up cake and towel jelly-roll style starting from a narrow end. Allow to cool on a wire rack.

5 Unroll cake and remove towel. Spread cherry pie filling over top of cake, leaving a 1-border, and roll it up again. Place on a serving platter, frost with whipped topping, and sprinkle with chocolate chips. Cover loosely and chill at least 1 hour, or until ready to serve.

Classic Coconut Layer Cake

Serves 12

1 (12- to 14-ounce) package shredded coconut, divided

1 (18.25-ounce) package white cake mix, batter prepared according to package directions

2 sticks unsalted butter, softened

2 cups confectioners' sugar

1 (6-ounce) package white baking bars, melted (see Tips)

1 Mix 2 cups coconut into cake batter and bake according to package directions for 2 (9-inch) round layers; let cool completely.

2 In a large bowl with an electric mixer on medium speed, beat butter, confectioners' sugar, and melted baking bars until fluffy and doubled in size. Add remaining coconut and mix until thoroughly combined.

3 Place 1 cake layer on a serving platter and frost top. Place second layer over first and frost top and sides. Cover loosely and chill at least 2 hours before serving.

Test Kitchen. Mr. Food Hints & Tips

To melt the white baking bars, in a microwaveable bowl, microwave 60 to 90 seconds, 30 seconds at a time, stirring until smooth. Oh, and if you'd like to use toasted coconut to kick up the flavor, go right ahead. (See page 63 for how to toast coconut.)

Mile-High Carrot Cake

Serves 12

Cake:

- 2 cups granulated sugar
- 1-1/2 cups vegetable oil
- 4 eggs
- 2 teaspoons baking soda
- 2 cups all-purpose flour
- 2 teaspoons ground cinnamon
- 1 teaspoon salt
- 1 cup shredded coconut
- 3 cups grated carrots (about 1 pound)
- 1 cup chopped walnuts

Cream Cheese Frosting:

- 1 (8-ounce) package cream cheese, softened
- 2 sticks butter, softened
- 1 teaspoon vanilla extract
- 4 cups confectioners' sugar

1 Preheat oven to 350 degrees F. Coat 2 (8-inch) round cake pans with cooking spray; lightly flour pans.

2 In a large bowl with an electric mixer, combine all cake ingredients, blending 30 seconds to 1 minute, or until a smooth, thick batter forms. DO NOT OVER-MIX! Pour batter evenly into prepared cake pans.

3 Bake 45 to 50 minutes, or until a toothpick inserted in center comes out clean and the tops are golden. Let cool completely. When cool, slice cakes horizontally in half, making 4 layers; set aside.

4 In a large bowl with an electric mixer, combine cream cheese and butter; mix well. Add vanilla; mix well. Gradually add confectioners' sugar, continuing to mix until well combined.

5 Place 1 cake layer on platter and evenly spread one-quarter of cream cheese frosting on top. Repeat with remaining cake layers and finish with cream cheese frosting on top. Serve immediately, or cover and chill until ready to serve.

Serving Suggestion:

To give this a fresh look, why not sprinkle the top of each slice with some grated carrots and a walnut half?

Shortcut German Chocolate Cake

Serves 12

1 (18.25-ounce) package chocolate cake mix, batter prepared according to package directions

1 cup chopped pecans, divided

1 cup shredded coconut, divided

1 cup sweetened condensed milk

3 tablespoons butter

1 teaspoon vanilla extract

1 Preheat oven to 375 degrees F. Coat a 9- x 13-inch baking dish with cooking spray, then lightly flour.

2 In a large bowl, combine cake batter, ½ cup pecans, and ½ cup coconut; mix well then pour into prepared baking dish.

3 Bake 30 to 35 minutes, or until a toothpick inserted in center comes out clean.

4 In a small saucepan over medium heat, combine sweetened condensed milk, butter, and vanilla. Cook about 5 minutes, or until thickened, stirring constantly. Stir in remaining pecans and remaining coconut. Spread over warm cake and allow cake to cool completely before cutting into squares.

Don't confuse canned sweetened condensed milk with canned evaporated milk; they're not interchangeable in recipes. Sweetened condensed milk adds sweetness and has a thicker texture, while evaporated milk is thin, with almost the consistency of skim milk.

Mom-Mom's Apple Cake

Serves 12

Cake:

- 3 apples
- 3 cups all-purpose flour
- 3 teaspoons baking powder
- ½ teaspoon salt
- 4 eggs
- 2 cups sugar
- 1 cup oil
- ⅓ cup orange juice
- 2-½ teaspoons vanilla extract

Topping: (mix and set aside)

- ⅔ cup sugar
- 1 teaspoon cinnamon

1 Preheat oven to 325 degrees F. Coat a Bundt pan with cooking spray and sprinkle with flour; set aside. Core, peel, and slice apples, and place into a bowl of cold water to prevent browning.

2 In a medium bowl, combine flour, baking powder, and salt. In a large bowl, beat eggs well; add sugar, oil, orange juice, and vanilla, beating well after each ingredient. Add flour mixture; mix well.

3 Pour ⅓ batter into prepared pan. Dry apples thoroughly, layer ½ over the batter, and sprinkle with ⅓ topping. Repeat with another layer. Add remaining batter, and sprinkle with remaining topping.

4 Bake 65 to 75 minutes, or until a toothpick in center comes out clean. Let cool about 2 hours, invert onto a platter.

Team Member Favorite:

This recipe has lots of meaning to Kelly from our Test Kitchen, as it was her grandmother's...or as she called her, her "Mom-Mom." Thank you Kelly for sharing this, Mom-Mom would be proud!

Banana Peanut Butter Cake

Serves 12

Cake:

1 cup granulated sugar

½ cup vegetable shortening

2 eggs

1 teaspoon baking soda

2 cups all-purpose flour

½ teaspoon salt

1 cup mashed banana
(about 3 ripe bananas)

1 teaspoon vanilla extract

Frosting:

4 ounces cream cheese, softened

½ cup creamy peanut butter

¾ stick butter, softened

3 cups confectioners' sugar

1 teaspoon vanilla extract

¼ cup chopped peanuts, for garnish

1 Preheat oven to 350 degrees F. Coat 2 (8-inch) round cake pans with cooking spray.

2 In a large bowl with an electric mixer, cream the granulated sugar and shortening until light and fluffy. Add eggs and beat thoroughly. Gradually blend in baking soda, flour, and salt. Beat in mashed banana and 1 teaspoon vanilla until thoroughly combined. Pour mixture into prepared cake pans.

3 Bake 25 to 30 minutes, or until a wooden toothpick inserted in center comes out clean. Let sit 5 minutes, then remove cakes from pans and place on a wire rack to cool.

4 In another bowl, combine cream cheese, peanut butter, and butter; beat until fluffy. Add confectioners' sugar and 1 teaspoon vanilla. Beat until thoroughly combined. Frost cake, then sprinkle with peanuts.

Chocolate Lava Cakes

Makes 6

1 cup semisweet
   chocolate chips

1-¼ sticks butter

½ cup all-purpose flour

1-½ cups confectioners' sugar

3 large eggs

3 egg yolks

1 teaspoon vanilla extract

1 Preheat oven to 425 degrees F. Coat 6 ramekins or custard cups with cooking spray (see Tips) and place on a baking sheet.

2 In a large microwaveable bowl, melt chocolate chips and butter in microwave 1 minute. Continue to melt at 15-second intervals until chocolate is smooth. Add flour and sugar to chocolate mixture; mix well. Stir in eggs and yolks until smooth, then stir in vanilla. Spoon batter evenly into ramekins.

3 Bake 12 to 14 minutes, or until edges are firm and center is soft; remove from oven and let sit 5 minutes. Loosen around edges with a knife and invert onto dessert plates.

If you don't have ramekins or custard cups, you can use a cupcake tin; just adjust cooking time accordingly. Top with a dollop of whipped cream or serve with a scoop of ice cream.

Lemon Coconut Cupcakes

Serves 24

- 1 (18.25-ounce) package lemon cake mix
- ½ cup lemon curd
- 1 (16-ounce) container vanilla frosting
- 1 teaspoon lemon extract
- 2 to 3 drops yellow food color
- 1 cup shredded coconut, toasted (see page 63 to learn how to toast coconut)

1 Preheat oven to 350 degrees F. Line 2 (12-cup) muffins tins with paper liners.

2 Prepare cake mix according to package directions. Spoon batter into prepared muffin tins, filling each cup about ⅓ full. Place ½ teaspoon lemon curd into center of batter in each cup. Top with a spoonful of batter. Bake according to package directions; cool completely.

3 Meanwhile, in a medium bowl, combine vanilla frosting, lemon extract, and yellow food color; mix well. Frost cooled cupcakes and sprinkle with toasted coconut.

Did You Know?
Lemon curd is a tart, yet sweet creamy spread that is perfect for adding extra-sunny flavor to baked goods and is usually available near the jams and jellies in the market.

Three-Minute Cupcakes

Makes 6

½ cup sugar

⅓ cup all-purpose flour

⅓ cup unsweetened cocoa powder

¼ teaspoon baking powder

1 egg

¼ cup mayonnaise

¼ cup milk

1 Line a microwaveable 6-cup muffin tin with paper liners, or place paper liners side by side in a microwaveable 7- x 11-inch baking dish.

2 In a medium bowl, combine all ingredients and mix until well blended.

3 Spoon mixture into paper liners and cook in microwave at 80 percent power 3 minutes or until a toothpick inserted into the center comes out clean. Remove cupcakes and let cool before serving.

You can make these really festive in no time by icing cooled cupcakes with store-bought frosting, then topping with colored sprinkles. Oh, make sure you use paper, not aluminum muffin liners in microwave oven.

Candy Bar-Stuffed Cupcakes

Makes 18

1- ½ sticks butter, melted
   and cooled

1 cup brown sugar

½ cup granulated sugar

1 tablespoon vanilla extract

2 eggs

2 cups all-purpose flour

½ teaspoon baking soda

12 miniature candy bars
   (see Tip below)

1 (16-ounce) container
   chocolate frosting

1 Preheat oven to 325 degrees F. Coat muffin tins with cooking spray.

2 In a large bowl with an electric mixer on medium speed, cream the butter, sugars, and vanilla until light and fluffy, 1 to 3 minutes. Add eggs and beat well.

3 In a medium bowl, whisk together flour and baking soda. Add to wet ingredients and beat on low speed just until incorporated. Scoop batter into prepared muffin tins, filling cups about 1/4 full. Top with candy bars. Spoon remaining batter on top of candy bars, filling cups about ½ full.

4 Bake 12 to 15 minutes, or until edges are golden. Let cool, remove from tins, then dollop each with frosting.

Test Kitchen Mr. Food Hints & Tips

We tried these with mini Butterfinger and mini Snickers bars, but when it comes to candy bars, it's fun to personalize these with your gang's favorites!

Fudgy "Cup" Cake Mix

Makes enough for 8 individual cupcakes

Cake Mix:

- 1 (18.25-ounce) package chocolate cake mix

- 1 (4-serving-size) package instant chocolate pudding and pie filling

Glaze Mix:

2-⅔ cups confectioners' sugar

¼ cup powdered dry hot cocoa mix

1 In a large bowl, combine dry cake and pudding mixes; blend well with a whisk.

2 In a medium bowl, combine confectioners' sugar and cocoa mix.

3 Divide cake mix evenly into 8 small plastic bags, about ½ cup each; seal and label "Cake Mix." Do the same with glaze mix, packing about ⅓ cup mix in each bag; seal and label "Glaze Mix."

To give Fudgy "Cup" Cake Mix as a gift: Place 1 sealed cake mix bag and 1 sealed glaze mix bag into a microwaveable mug, and attach the recipe for Making a Fudgy "Cup" Cake (below).

To bake a Fudgy "Cup" Cake: Spray inside of a microwaveable mug generously with cooking spray. Pour prepared bag of cake mix into mug. Add 1 egg, 1 tablespoon vegetable oil, and 1 tablespoon water. Mix until all ingredients are combined. Microwave at 100% power about 2 minutes, or until cake is set. Meanwhile, place prepared bag of glaze mix in a small bowl and add 1-1/2 teaspoons milk; mix well then pour glaze over mug cake immediately after removing it from microwave. Serve cake warm in the mug.

Banana Split Cupcakes

Makes 12

- 1 (14-ounce) package banana bread muffin mix
- 1 (16-ounce) container vanilla frosting
- ½ cup hot fudge
- ½ cup chopped walnuts
- 12 maraschino cherries

1 Preheat oven according to package directions. Line a muffin tin with paper liners.

2 Make muffin mix according to package directions. Spoon batter into muffin tin, filling each cup about 3/4 full.

3 Bake according to package directions; let cool completely.

4 Spread frosting over each cupcake, drizzle with hot fudge, sprinkle with nuts, and top each with a cherry.

Serving Suggestion:
When you are at the market, pick up some dried banana chips and garnish each cupcake with a few slices. How fun will that look?

Surprise Cheesecake Cupcakes

Makes 30

1 (18.25-ounce) package chocolate cake mix

1 (8-ounce) package cream cheese, softened

⅓ cup sugar

1 egg

1 cup chocolate chips

1 Preheat oven to 350 degrees F. Line muffin tins with paper liners.

2 Prepare cake mix according to package directions. Spoon batter into muffin cups, filling each about 2/3 full.

3 In a large bowl, beat cream cheese and sugar until light and fluffy. Beat in egg, then stir in chocolate chips. Drop 1 teaspoon cheese mixture onto each cupcake.

4 Bake according to cake mix package directions. Let cool and keep refrigerated until ready to serve.

Brownies & Bars

Triple Chocolate Brownie Surprise

Makes 16

1 (19.8-ounce) package
   brownie mix

2 eggs

¼ cup vegetable oil

1 (¾-cup) scoop cookies and
   cream ice cream, softened

¼ cup hot fudge topping
   (room temperature)

16-20 chocolate cream sandwich
   cookies (enough to make a
   layer in the pan)

1 Preheat oven to 350 degrees F. Coat an 8-inch-square baking dish with cooking spray.

2 In a large bowl, combine brownie mix, eggs, and oil, but do not add the water called for on the package. Add ice cream and hot fudge to brownie batter and stir to combine. Pour half the brownie batter into prepared baking dish. Place a layer of whole sandwich cookies over batter, then top with remaining batter.

3 Bake 45 to 50 minutes, or until a toothpick inserted in center comes out clean.

Serving Suggestion:
These will be over-the-top good served with the leftover cookies and cream ice cream and topped with hot fudge.

Mocha-Topped Brownies

Makes 9

- 3 (1-ounce) squares unsweetened chocolate
- 1 stick butter
- 1 cup sugar
- 2 eggs, beaten
- ⅔ cup all-purpose flour
- Pinch of salt
- 1 teaspoon vanilla extract
- 1 cup chopped walnuts or other nuts (optional)
- 1 (16-ounce) container cream cheese frosting
- 2 teaspoons unsweetened cocoa powder
- 1 tablespoon strong black coffee, cooled (see Tip)

1. Preheat oven to 350 degrees F. Coat an 8-inch-square baking dish with cooking spray.

2. In a large microwaveable bowl, microwave chocolate and butter 1 to 1½ minutes, or until melted. Remove from heat and transfer to a large bowl. Beat in sugar and eggs. Stir in flour, salt, and vanilla until well blended. Stir in nuts, if desired. Pour batter into prepared baking dish.

3. Bake 30 to 35 minutes, or until toothpick inserted in center comes out clean. Let cool.

4. In a medium bowl, combine remaining ingredients; mix until smooth, then frost brownies.

To make really strong black coffee, which gives these a true mocha taste, we recommend mixing a teaspoon of instant coffee or espresso powder with a tablespoon of water until it's dissolved.

Minty Brownies

Serves 15

- 1 (19.8-ounce) package brownie mix, batter prepared according to package directions
- 1 (16-ounce) container vanilla frosting
- 1 tablespoon mint extract
- 2 to 3 drops green food color
- ½ cup semisweet chocolate chips, melted

1. Bake brownie batter in a 9- x 13-inch baking dish according to package directions. Allow to cool completely.

2. In a medium bowl, combine frosting, mint extract, and green food color; mix well. Spread over brownies.

3. Using a fork, drizzle melted chocolate in a criss-cross pattern over frosted brownies. Allow chocolate to set, then cut into bars and serve.

Did You Know?
Package sizes of brownie mix vary from brand to brand, usually between 18 and 21 ounces. After testing several recipes, we feel that most national brands are interchangeable.

Blue Ribbon Brownies

Makes 24

3 sticks butter

3 cups sugar

5 eggs

2 teaspoons vanilla extract

1-¼ cups all-purpose flour

1-¼ cups unsweetened cocoa powder

1 teaspoon salt

2 cups chopped walnuts

1. Preheat oven to 350 degrees F. Coat a 9- x 13-inch baking dish with cooking spray.

2. In a large saucepan over medium heat, melt butter. Stir in sugar until dissolved. Remove mixture from heat and let cool slightly. Beat in eggs, one at a time, mixing well after each addition. Stir in vanilla.

3. Sift flour, cocoa, and salt together. Add flour mixture to butter mixture, mixing until combined. Stir in walnuts. Spread batter into prepared baking dish.

4. Bake 30 to 35 minutes, or until a toothpick inserted in center comes out clean.

We found that dark-colored pans can cause overbrowning, so we recommend aluminum baking pans or glass baking dishes.

Cheesecake Brownie Bars

Makes 16

2 (8-ounce) packages cream cheese, softened

2 eggs

2 tablespoons sugar

1 teaspoon vanilla extract

1 (19.8-ounce) package brownie mix, batter prepared according to package directions

1 Preheat oven to 350 degrees F. Coat a 9- x 13-inch baking dish with cooking spray; set aside.

2 In a medium bowl with an electric mixer on medium speed, combine cream cheese, eggs, sugar, and vanilla until fluffy.

3 Spread half the brownie batter into prepared baking dish. Spoon cream cheese mixture over batter then top with remaining half of batter. Using a knife, cut through batter, swirling to create a marbled effect.

4 Bake 35 to 40 minutes, or until a toothpick inserted in center comes out clean. Allow to cool, then cut into bars and serve, or cover and chill until ready to serve.

Cookie 'n' Coffee Brownies

Makes 24

1 (16.5-ounce) roll refrigerated sugar cookie dough

2 eggs, lightly beaten

1 (19.8-ounce) package brownie mix

½ cup vegetable oil

⅓ cup strong black coffee, cooled

1 cup semisweet chocolate chips

1 Preheat oven to 350 degrees F. Press cookie dough into bottom of a 9- x 13-inch baking dish; set aside.

2 In a large bowl, combine eggs, brownie mix, oil, and coffee until just combined. Spread batter over cookie dough. Sprinkle with chocolate chips.

3 Bake 40 minutes, or until edges are set and toothpick inserted in center comes out clean. Cool in pan on a wire rack. Cut into squares and serve.

We think these are pretty good as is, but discovered if we sprinkle the batter with some mini M&M's or some chopped-up toffee candy pieces before baking, they're even better!

Hot Fudge Brownies

Serves 6

1 cup all-purpose flour

¾ cup granulated sugar

¼ cup plus 2 tablespoons
  unsweetened cocoa powder,
  divided

2 teaspoons baking powder

½ teaspoon salt

½ cup milk

2 tablespoons vegetable oil

1 teaspoon vanilla extract

¾ cup chopped walnuts
  (optional)

¾ cup packed light brown sugar

1-¾ cups hot water

1. Preheat oven to 350 degrees F. Coat an 8-inch-square baking dish with cooking spray.

2. In a large bowl, combine flour, granulated sugar, 2 tablespoons cocoa, the baking powder, and salt. Add milk, oil and vanilla; mix with a spoon until smooth. Stir in walnuts, if desired, and pour batter into prepared baking dish.

3. In a small bowl, combine brown sugar and remaining cocoa; sprinkle evenly over batter. Pour hot water over brown sugar and cocoa.

4. Bake 35 to 40 minutes, or until top is cracked and brownies are just firm to the touch. Remove from oven and let cool 15 minutes before serving.

Serving Suggestion:

How about topping each brownie with a scoop of vanilla ice cream before spooning the fudge sauce from the pan over the top?

Pretzel-Crusted Hazelnut Brownies

Makes 16

2-½ cups pretzels

⅓ cup brown sugar

¾ stick butter, melted

1 stick butter, softened

1 cup granulated sugar

2 eggs

¾ teaspoon vanilla extract

¼ teaspoon salt

⅓ cup hazelnut-chocolate spread (like Nutella)

¼ cup unsweetened cocoa powder

⅔ cup all-purpose flour

1 Preheat oven to 350 degrees F. Lightly coat an 8-inch square baking dish with cooking spray; set aside.

2 To make the crust, place pretzels in a food processor and pulse until coarsely crushed. Add brown sugar and melted butter; pulsing until combined. Press pretzel mixture firmly into prepared baking dish.

3 Bake 12 to 15 minutes, or until edges are golden.

4 Meanwhile, in a medium bowl, cream softened butter and granulated sugar together. Add eggs and blend well. Add vanilla, salt, and hazelnut-chocolate spread; mix until combined. Add cocoa and flour; mix until combined but don't overbeat. Pour over pretzel crust.

5 Bake 20 to 25 minutes, or until a toothpick inserted in center comes out clean. Cut into squares and serve.

Did You Know?

You can make a crust out of not only crushed pretzels mixed with butter, but crushed cookie crumbs or crushed cereal, as well.

No-Bake Marshmallow Fudgies

Makes 36

2 cups semisweet chocolate chips

1 cup plus 2 teaspoons evaporated milk, divided

1 (18-ounce) package chocolate chip cookies

2 cups miniature marshmallows

1 cup chopped pecans

1 cup confectioners' sugar

1 Coat a 9- x 13-inch baking dish with cooking spray.

2 In a large heavy saucepan, combine chocolate chips and 1 cup evaporated milk; cook over low heat until chocolate melts, stirring occasionally. Set aside.

3 Meanwhile, in a food processor, process chocolate chip cookies in 2 batches to make coarse crumbs. Place crumbs in a large bowl.

4 Stir marshmallows, pecans, and confectioners' sugar into cookie crumbs. Reserve ½ cup chocolate mixture; set aside. Stir remaining chocolate mixture into crumb mixture. Press into prepared baking dish.

5 Combine reserved chocolate mixture and reserved evaporated milk in a small bowl; spread over crumb mixture. Cover and chill at least 1 hour. Cut into squares.

Old-Fashioned Citrus Bars

Makes 15

2-½ cups all-purpose flour, divided

2 sticks butter, softened

1 cup confectioners' sugar, plus extra for topping

2 cups granulated sugar

4 eggs

½ cup lemon juice

2 tablespoons lime zest

1 teaspoon lemon extract

1 Preheat oven to 350 degrees F.

2 In a medium bowl, combine 2 cups flour, the butter, and 1 cup confectioners' sugar; mix until crumbly. Press into bottom of a 9- x 13-inch baking dish to form a crust. Bake 15 minutes.

3 Meanwhile, in a large bowl with an electric mixer on medium speed, beat remaining flour, the granulated sugar, eggs, lemon juice, lime zest, and lemon extract until well blended. Pour over hot crust.

4 Bake 25 to 30 minutes, or until set. Allow to cool, then cut into bars. Dust with extra confectioners' sugar and serve.

Did You Know?
Lemon juice is known to be a good digestive aid, an immunity booster, and even makes our skin look healthier.

Peanut Butter & Jelly Bars

Makes 15

2-¼ cups all-purpose flour

1 stick butter, melted

½ cup creamy peanut butter

½ cup packed light brown sugar

¼ cup granulated sugar

1 egg

1 cup strawberry jelly or preserves (see note)

1. Preheat oven to 350 degrees F. Coat a 9- x 13-inch baking dish with cooking spray.

2. In a large bowl, combine all ingredients except jelly. Beat with an electric mixer on medium speed 2 minutes, or until blended and crumbly.

3. Reserve 1 cup of mixture. Spread remaining mixture over bottom of prepared baking dish, then spread jelly evenly over it. Crumble reserved mixture over top.

4. Bake 35 to 40 minutes, or until topping is golden. Allow to cool completely, then cut into bars and serve.

Lighten It Up:
Sure, not only can you switch up the flavor of jam or jelly...you can also use a sugar-free variety as well. Every bit helps.

Confetti Chocolate Bars

Makes 24

2 cups semisweet chocolate chips

1 (8-ounce) package cream cheese, softened

1 (5-ounce) can evaporated milk

½ cup chopped walnuts

1 cup mini chocolate-covered candies

1-½ teaspoons vanilla extract, divided

3 cups all-purpose flour

1-½ cups sugar

1 teaspoon baking powder

½ teaspoon salt

2 sticks butter, softened

2 eggs

1 Preheat oven to 350 degrees F.

2 In a saucepan, combine chocolate chips, cream cheese, and evaporated milk. Cook over low heat, stirring constantly, until chips are melted and mixture is smooth. Remove from heat and let cool slightly. Stir in walnuts, chocolate-covered candies, and 1 teaspoon vanilla; set aside.

3 In a large bowl, combine flour, sugar, baking powder, salt, butter, eggs, and remaining vanilla. Beat with an electric mixer on low speed until mixture resembles coarse crumbs.

4 Press half the crumb mixture into an ungreased 9- x 13-inch baking dish. Spread chocolate mixture over crumb mixture. Top with remaining crumb mixture.

5 Bake 35 to 40 minutes, or until golden. Cool, then cut into bars.

Chocolate Salted Caramel Bars

Makes 24

2 (16.5-ounce) rolls refrigerated chocolate chip cookie dough

36 caramel squares, unwrapped

3 tablespoons heavy cream

Sea salt for sprinkling

1 Preheat oven to 350 degrees F. Coat a 9- x 13-inch baking dish with cooking spray.

2 Slice cookie dough rolls into 1/4-inch slices. Arrange slices from one roll on bottom of prepared baking dish; press together so there are no holes in dough.

3 In a large microwaveable bowl, combine caramels and heavy cream. Microwave on high until caramels are melted, stirring every 30 seconds. This will take about 2 minutes. Pour caramel mixture evenly over dough; sprinkle with sea salt and top with remaining slices of cookie dough. Sprinkle with additional sea salt.

4 Bake 35 to 40 minutes, or until golden and center is slightly firm. Remove from oven, let cool slightly, then refrigerate until well chilled. Cut into slices and serve.

Make sure you keep your cookie dough refrigerated until just before slicing. That way it will slice easier. Yes, it's these little tricks that make our time in the kitchen that much easier.

Ooey-Gooey Turtle Bars

Makes 24

1 (16.5-ounce) roll refrigerated sugar cookie dough

2 cups semisweet chocolate chips

1 (12-ounce) jar caramel topping

1 cup coarsely chopped pecans

1 Preheat oven to 350 degrees F.

2 Press cookie dough into bottom of 9- x 13-inch baking dish. Sprinkle with chocolate chips, drizzle with caramel topping, and sprinkle with pecans.

3 Bake 18 to 20 minutes, or until chips melt; cool completely in baking dish on wire rack. Chill at least 2 hours; cut into bars.

Pecan Blondies

Makes 12

1 stick butter, softened

2 cups packed dark brown sugar

2 eggs, well beaten

1 cup all-purpose flour

1 teaspoon baking powder

1 teaspoon vanilla extract

1 cup pecan pieces

½ cup butterscotch chips

Confectioners' sugar for sprinkling (optional)

1 Preheat oven to 350 degrees F. Coat an 8-inch-square baking dish with cooking spray.

2 In a large bowl with an electric mixer on medium speed, cream softened butter; add brown sugar and eggs. Mix thoroughly, then add flour and baking powder; blend well. Stir in vanilla, nuts, and butterscotch chips, then pour batter into prepared baking dish.

3 Bake 35 to 40 minutes, or until toothpick inserted in center comes out clean. Cool in pan, then cut into squares and sprinkle with confectioners' sugar, if desired.

Did You Know?

All of our recipes are tested, tasted, and tested again and again. This is our way of ensuring foolproof recipes every time.

Crispy Cereal Bars

Makes 12

½ stick butter

1 (16-ounce) bag mini marshmallows

8 cups cereal of your choice (see Tips)

1 Coat a 9- x 13-inch baking dish with cooking spray.

2 Place butter and marshmallows in a large microwaveable glass bowl and microwave 1 to 2 minutes to melt; stir well. Mix in cereal and stir. Pour mixture into prepared baking dish and press down with a spoon. Cut into bars and serve.

We tested these with both Fruit Loops and Apple Jacks, but feel free to use your favorite breakfast cereal. Also, we suggest spraying your spoon with cooking spray before using it to press down the mixture, as that will prevent it from sticking.

White Chocolate Hawaiian Bars

Makes 15

- 1 (16.5-ounce) roll refrigerated sugar cookie dough, divided
- 3 (8-ounce) packages cream cheese, softened
- 3 eggs
- ¾ cup sugar
- 1 teaspoon vanilla extract
- 2 cups white chocolate chips
- 1 cup coarsely chopped macadamia nuts
- ½ cup shredded coconut

1 Preheat oven to 350 degrees F. Coat a 9- x 13-inch baking dish with cooking spray.

2 Press two-thirds of the cookie dough into bottom of prepared baking dish.

3 In a large bowl with an electric mixer on medium speed, beat cream cheese, eggs, sugar, and vanilla until creamy. Stir in chocolate chips and nuts and pour into prepared baking dish.

4 Crumble remaining cookie dough and sprinkle evenly over cream cheese mixture. Sprinkle coconut over top.

5 Bake 40 to 45 minutes, or until crust is golden and center is set. Allow to cool completely, then cover and chill at least 4 hours. Cut into bars and serve.

When baking brownies or bars like these, make sure you bake them on the middle rack so the top and bottom bake evenly. Too high and coconut will burn, too low and the sugar cookie crust will over bake.

Peanut Butter-Bacon Bars

Makes 16

1 cup packed light brown sugar

1 stick butter, softened

½ cup peanut butter

1 egg

1 teaspoon vanilla extract

1-½ cups all-purpose flour

1 teaspoon baking soda

¼ teaspoon salt

10 bacon slices, crisply cooked,
   then crumbled, divided

½ cup chopped peanuts, divided

1 cup semi-sweet chocolate chips

1 Preheat oven to 350 degrees F. Coat an 8-inch-square baking dish with cooking spray.

2 In a large bowl with an electric mixer on medium speed, beat brown sugar and butter until creamy. Beat in peanut butter, egg, and vanilla. Add flour, baking soda, and salt; mix well. Stir in half the bacon and 1/3 cup peanuts. Spread into prepared baking dish.

3 Bake 20 to 25 minutes, or until a toothpick inserted in center comes out clean. Remove from oven and sprinkle evenly with chocolate chips. Return to oven and bake 1 additional minute. Immediately spread melted chocolate chips over top. Sprinkle with remaining bacon and peanuts. Let cool completely, then cut into squares.

Lighten It Up:

Ok, these aren't exactly a health bar but if you are looking for a version that makes you feel less guilty, we suggested replacing the bacon with imitation bacon bits. And by-the-way, turkey bacon will not work well here.

Key Lime Coconut Bars

Makes 16

1-½ cups finely crushed coconut cookies

3 tablespoons butter, melted

1 (8-ounce) package cream cheese, softened

1 (14-ounce) can sweetened condensed milk

¼ cup lime juice

1 tablespoon lime zest

1. Preheat oven to 350 degrees F. Coat an 8-inch-square baking dish with cooking spray.

2. In a bowl, combine cookie crumbs and butter thoroughly with a fork. Press evenly into bottom of prepared baking dish.

3. In a small bowl with an electric mixer on medium speed, beat cream cheese until light and fluffy. Gradually beat in sweetened condensed milk until smooth. Beat in lime juice and zest. Spread over cookie crumb crust .

4. Bake about 35 minutes, or until center is set. Cool 30 minutes, then chill at least 3 hours before cutting into bars and serving.

Serving Suggestion:

Since we eat with our eyes, why not top each bar with some shredded toasted coconut or a sprinkle of lime zest?

Kitchen Sink Cookie Bars

Makes 18

1 stick butter, softened

¾ cup sugar

2 eggs

1 teaspoon vanilla extract

¾ cup all-purpose flour

½ cup chopped pecans

2 tablespoons unsweetened cocoa powder

¼ teaspoon baking powder

¼ teaspoon salt

2 cups miniature marshmallows

1 cup semisweet chocolate chips

1 cup crunchy peanut butter

1-½ cups crispy rice cereal

1 Preheat oven to 350 degrees F. Coat a 9- x 13-inch baking dish with cooking spray.

2 In a large bowl, cream butter and sugar with an electric mixer, then beat in eggs and vanilla.

3 In a separate bowl, combine flour, pecans, cocoa, baking powder, and salt; add to butter mixture, blending thoroughly. Spread mixture into prepared baking dish.

4 Bake 15 to 20 minutes, or until a toothpick inserted in center comes out clean. Sprinkle marshmallows evenly over top and bake an additional 3 minutes. Remove from oven to cool.

5 Meanwhile, in a small saucepan over low heat, melt chocolate chips and peanut butter together; remove from heat and stir in cereal. Spread mixture over cooled uncut bars. Chill, then cut into bars. Keep refrigerated.

Almond Lovers' Toffee Bars

Makes 20

1-½ cups all-purpose flour

½ cup confectioners' sugar

1-½ cups finely chopped almonds, divided

1-½ sticks cold butter

1 (14-ounce) can sweetened condensed milk

1 egg, beaten

1 teaspoon almond extract

6 (1.4-ounce) chocolate-covered toffee candy bars, coarsely chopped

1 Preheat oven to 350 degrees F.

2 In a medium bowl, combine flour, confectioners' sugar, and ½-cup chopped almonds. Using 2 knives in a scissor-like fashion, cut butter into mixture until crumbly, then press firmly into bottom of a 9- x 13-inch baking dish. Bake 15 minutes.

3 Meanwhile, in a large bowl, combine sweetened condensed milk, egg, and almond extract; mix well. Stir in chopped candy bars and remaining chopped almonds, then spread evenly over crust.

4 Bake 22 to 25 minutes, or until golden. Let cool; cover and chill, then cut into bars when ready to serve.

Don't think you're the only person who gets sweetened condensed milk and evaporated milk mixed up. Yes, they both come in cans, but are very different and are not interchangeable. Sweetened condensed milk is much sweeter and thicker than evaporated.

Nutty Chocolate "Bars"

Makes 24

2 sticks butter, melted

4 cups quick-cooking oats

1 cup brown sugar

¾ cup coarsely chopped peanuts

1-½ cups peanut butter

2 cups chocolate chips

1 Preheat oven to 350 degrees F. Coat an 11- x 15-inch rimmed baking sheet with cooking spray.

2 In a large bowl, mix together butter, oats, brown sugar, and peanuts. Spread batter into prepared pan.

3 Bake 15 to 18 minutes, or until a toothpick inserted in center comes out clean. Let cool 5 minutes, then spread peanut butter over top.

4 In a microwaveable bowl, melt chocolate chips 1- to 1-1/2 minutes or until melted, stirring until smooth. Drizzle chocolate over peanut butter and refrigerate 15 minutes. Cut into bars.

Did You Know?
While triple-testing this recipe, one comment we heard over and over again from our Team, was that they tasted like their favorite candy bar. What do you think?

Toffee Apple Squares

Makes 16

1 (16.5-ounce) roll refrigerated sugar cookie dough

1 (8-ounce) package cream cheese, softened

½ cup packed brown sugar

¼ cup peanut butter

½ teaspoon vanilla extract

1 (14.5-ounce) can sliced apples in water, drained

¼ cup caramel topping

½ cup peanuts, chopped

1 Preheat oven to 350 degrees F. Press cookie dough into bottom of a 9- x 13-inch baking dish.

2 Bake 16-18 minutes, or until light golden brown. Remove from oven; cool 10 minutes.

3 Meanwhile, in a medium bowl, combine cream cheese, brown sugar, peanut butter, and vanilla; mix well. Spread cream cheese mixture evenly over cookie, then arrange apples evenly over that.

4 Microwave caramel topping 20 to 30 seconds, or until warm; drizzle evenly over apples. Sprinkle with peanuts Let cool then cut into squares.

Did You Know?

Caramels were first introduced to the masses in the late 1800's. Soon after, the concept of dipping tart apples into melted caramels is believed to have become popular as a way to balance out its sweetness. What a great invention, huh?

Notes

Pies

Caramel Peanut Pumpkin Pie

Serves 8

1 refrigerated rolled pie crust
(from a 15-ounce package)

1 (15-ounce) can 100% pure
pumpkin (not pie filling)

2 eggs, slightly beaten

¾ cup sugar

½ teaspoon salt

1-½ teaspoons all-purpose flour

1-½ teaspoons pumpkin pie spice

1-¼ teaspoons ground cinnamon

1 (12-ounce) can evaporated milk

1 (8-ounce) container frozen
whipped topping, thawed

¼ cup caramel sauce

¼ cup salted peanuts, coarsely
chopped

1 Preheat oven to 425 degrees F. Unroll pie crust and place in a 9-inch pie plate, pressing crust firmly into plate; flute edges and set aside.

2 In a large bowl, mix together pumpkin, eggs, sugar, salt, flour, pumpkin pie spice, cinnamon, and evaporated milk; pour mixture into pie crust.

3 Bake 20 minutes, then reduce heat to 350 degrees and bake an additional 40 minutes, or until a knife inserted in center comes out clean.

4 Let cool completely, then top with whipped topping, drizzle with caramel sauce, and sprinkle with chopped peanuts.

The pie filling will look low in the shell when it comes out of the oven but don't worry! It'll be just right once it's topped with the whipped topping and the peanuts! And, if you don't have pumpkin pie spice, you can use a mixture of ½ teaspoon ground ginger, ½ teaspoon ground nutmeg, and ¼ teaspoon ground cloves.

Crustless Lemon Coconut Pie

Serves 8

1 (14-ounce) can sweetened
condensed milk

1 cup water

½ cup lemon juice

½ cup pancake and biscuit mix
(like Bisquick)

3 eggs

½ stick butter, softened

1-½ teaspoons vanilla extract

1 cup shredded coconut

1 Preheat oven to 350 degrees F. Coat a 9-inch deep dish pie plate with cooking spray.

2 In a blender, combine all ingredients except coconut; blend on low speed 1 minute. Pour mixture into prepared pie plate; let stand 5 minutes. Sprinkle coconut over top.

3 Bake 40 to 45 minutes, or until a knife inserted in center comes out clean. Let cool. Refrigerate until ready to serve.

Mocha Cream Pie

Serves 8

- 1 (4-serving-size) package instant chocolate pudding and pie filling
- 1-¾ cups milk
- 1 (.25-ounce) envelope unflavored gelatin
- 3 tablespoons hot water
- ¼ cup plus 2 teaspoons coffee liqueur, divided
- 1 (9-inch) frozen ready-to-bake deep-dish pie shell, baked according to package directions and cooled
- 1 cup (½ pint) heavy cream
- 2 tablespoons sugar

1 In a medium bowl, whisk pudding mix and milk until thickened.

2 In a small bowl, combine gelatin and hot water and beat with a fork until completely dissolved. Add to pudding mixture along with ¼ cup coffee liqueur; mix well. Pour into pie shell and refrigerate 2 hours, or until pie is firm.

3 In a medium bowl with an electric mixer on medium speed, beat cream and sugar 2 to 4 minutes, or until soft peaks form. Add remaining coffee liqueur and beat until stiff peaks form. Spread whipped cream over pie. Serve immediately or cover and chill until ready to serve.

Heavy cream whips up best if made in a chilled bowl with chilled beaters. So if you can, put the bowl and beaters in the refrigerator for about a half-hour before whipping.

Plantation Peachy Pie

Serves 8

½ cup plus 1 tablespoon sugar, divided

½ teaspoon cinnamon

5 large ripe peaches, sliced

¼ cup all-purpose flour

3 tablespoons butter, melted

1 teaspoon vanilla extract

1 (15-ounce) package refrigerated rolled pie crust

1 egg

1 Preheat oven to 375 degrees F. In a small bowl, mix ½ cup sugar and the cinnamon; reserve 1 tablespoon for garnish.

2 In a large bowl, combine peaches, flour, butter, vanilla, and cinnamon-sugar mixture; mix well. Unroll one pie crust and place in a 9-inch pie plate, pressing crust firmly into plate. Spoon peach mixture into crust.

3 Unroll remaining pie crust and place over peach mixture. Pinch together and trim the edges to seal and flute. Cut slits in the top, brush with egg, and sprinkle with reserved cinnamon-sugar mixture.

4 Bake 35 to 40 minutes, or until golden and bubbly. Let cool and serve.

When fresh peaches are not bountiful, no worries, you can always substitute frozen sliced peaches for the fresh.

Ice Cream Cone Pie

Serves 8

12 sugar ice cream cones

1 cup coarsely chopped toasted pecans

½ cup chocolate chips

5 tablespoons butter

½ gallon any flavor ice cream, softened

1 Place the sugar cones in a resealable plastic bag and crush into small pieces with a rolling pin. (Do not chop in food processor.) In a medium bowl, mix crushed cones and pecans; set aside.

2 In a small saucepan over low heat, melt chocolate chips and butter, stirring occasionally. Pour over cone mixture, mixing well, and press half the mixture evenly over bottom and up the sides of an ungreased 9-inch pie plate. Spread ice cream into the crust. Sprinkle remaining cone mixture over top of pie, and press down with the back of a spoon.

3 Cover and freeze several hours, or until firm. Pie may be kept frozen up to 1 month.

Did You Know?
Toasting pecans in a skillet for 3 to 4 minutes brings out more of their flavor. Be sure to stir frequently to keep them from burning.

Turtle Pudding Pie

Serves 8

1 (8-ounce) package cream cheese, softened

1 (4-serving-size) package instant chocolate pudding and pie filling

½ cup milk

1 (8-ounce) container frozen whipped topping, thawed, divided

1 (9-inch) chocolate graham cracker pie crust

4 tablespoons caramel topping, divided

¼ cup coarsely chopped pecans

1 In a large bowl, with an electric mixer on medium speed, beat cream cheese 2 to 3 minutes, or until creamy. Slowly add pudding mix and milk and continue beating until smooth. Fold in 2 cups whipped topping and stir until well blended. Spoon into pie crust.

2 Drizzle with 3 tablespoons caramel topping and use a knife to swirl it into the cream cheese mixture.

3 Completely cover top of pie with remaining whipped topping. Drizzle with remaining caramel topping, sprinkle with chopped pecans, and freeze 15 minutes. Serve, or cover and refrigerate until ready to serve.

Toasted Coconut Cream Pie

Serves 8

2 cups milk

3 eggs

1-¼ cups shredded coconut, toasted, divided (see Tip)

½ cup sugar

6 tablespoons all-purpose flour

1 tablespoon butter

1 teaspoon vanilla extract

⅛ teaspoon salt

1 (9-inch) frozen ready-to-bake pie shell, baked according to package directions and cooled

2 cups frozen whipped topping, thawed

1. In a medium saucepan, whisk together milk, eggs, 1 cup coconut, sugar, flour, butter, vanilla, and salt. Cook over medium heat 5 to 7 minutes, or until thickened, stirring occasionally. Pour into pie shell.

2. Chill at least 4 hours, or until set. Spread whipped topping over pie, sprinkle with remaining coconut and serve, or cover and keep chilled until ready to serve.

Test Kitchen Mr. Food Hints & Tips

To toast coconut, spread it on a rimmed baking sheet and bake at 350 degrees, stirring once or twice, until golden, about 5 to 10 minutes. Keep an eye on it so it doesn't burn. Believe us... we learn the hard way!

White Russian Pie

Serves 8

24 large marshmallows

½ cup milk

21 cream-filled chocolate sandwich cookies, finely crushed

3 tablespoons butter, melted

2 cups whipped cream or whipped topping

⅓ cup coffee liqueur or strong black coffee, chilled

Chocolate curls (optional)

1 In a medium saucepan, combine marshmallows and milk; cook over low heat until marshmallows are melted, stirring constantly. Let cool in pan 15 minutes; set aside.

2 Meanwhile, in a medium bowl, combine cookie crumbs and butter; mix well then press mixture firmly over bottom and sides of a 9-inch pie plate. Freeze 15 minutes, or until firm.

3 Place whipped cream in a large bowl. Stir liqueur into marshmallow mixture, then gently fold into whipped cream; spoon into crust and cover loosely.

4 Freeze pie 8 hours, or until firm. Just before serving, garnish with chocolate curls, if desired.

Serving Suggestion:
Finish this off with chocolate curls by simply using a vegetable peeler on a room-temperature chocolate bar. Maybe mix dark and white chocolate bars to really fancy it up?

Four-Layer Pecan Pie

Serves 8

- 1 refrigerated rolled pie crust (from a 15-ounce package)
- 1 (8-ounce) package cream cheese, softened
- ½ cup sugar, divided
- 2 teaspoons vanilla extract, divided
- 4 eggs
- 1 cup corn syrup
- 1-¼ cups chopped pecans

1. Preheat oven to 375 degrees F. Unroll pie crust and place in a 9-inch deep dish pie plate, pressing crust firmly into plate.

2. In a medium bowl with an electric mixer on low speed, beat cream cheese, ¼ cup sugar, 1 teaspoon vanilla, and 1 egg, until smooth; set aside.

3. In another medium bowl, beat 3 eggs. Add remaining sugar, the corn syrup, and remaining vanilla; mix well.

4. Spread cream cheese mixture in pie crust. Sprinkle with pecans and slowly pour corn syrup mixture over pecans.

5. Bake 40 to 45 minutes, or until center is set. Let cool, then refrigerate 4 hours or until ready to serve.

Did You Know?

This is one of our most popular TV pie recipes ever, so we just HAD to include it here!

Very Berry Pie

Serves 8

1 refrigerated rolled pie crust (from a 15-ounce package)

1 (4-serving-size) package blackberry or blueberry gelatin

½ cup sugar

¼ cup cornstarch

¾ cup ginger ale

1-½ cups blackberries, divided

1-½ cups raspberries, divided

1-½ cups blueberries, divided

1 Unroll pie crust and place in a 9-inch pie plate, pressing crust firmly into plate; flute edges and bake according to package directions.

2 In a medium saucepan over medium heat, combine gelatin, sugar, cornstarch, ginger ale, and ½ cup each of blackberries, raspberries, and blueberries. Cook 5 to 6 minutes, or until berries have broken apart and mixture has thickened, stirring frequently. Remove from heat and let cool about 5 minutes.

3 Stir in remaining berries and spoon into pie crust.

4 Chill at least 4 hours, or until set. Serve, or cover and keep chilled until ready to serve.

Feel free to mix and match the types of berries you use. If you want to add strawberries, go right ahead, just make sure they are sliced so they mix in evenly. Oh, and if you want to make this with a homemade crust, try our Prize-Winning Pie Crust on page 77.

Banana Split Cream Pie

Serves 8

1 (4-serving-size) package cook-
   and-serve vanilla pudding mix

1 cup half-and-half

1 large ripe banana, peeled and
   sliced

1 (9-inch) graham cracker pie crust

1 (8-ounce) container frozen
   whipped topping, thawed, divided

¼ cup sliced almonds

8 maraschino cherries

1 In a medium saucepan, combine pudding mix and half-and-half; cook over medium heat until thickened, stirring constantly. Remove from heat. Spoon into a medium bowl, cover surface with wax paper, and let cool to room temperature.

2 Meanwhile, place banana slices on bottom of pie crust. Fold half the whipped topping into the cooled pudding. Spoon pudding mixture evenly over bananas then spoon remaining whipped topping over pudding mixture. Top with almonds and cherries.

3 Cover and chill at least 4 hours, or until ready to serve.

Serving Suggestion:
What do you like on your banana split? Hot Fudge? Pineapple topping? Whatever your preference is, feel free to top each slice of pie to make it your very own creation.

Frozen Mississippi Mud Pie

Serves 8

1 quart coffee ice cream, softened (see Tip)

1 (9-inch) chocolate crumb pie crust

1-¼ cups hot fudge topping, slightly warmed, divided

1 (8-ounce) container frozen whipped topping, thawed

Chopped nuts for sprinkling (optional)

1 Spoon softened ice cream into pie crust. Freeze until firm, about 2 hours.

2 Top with 1 cup hot fudge and the whipped topping, drizzle with remaining hot fudge, and sprinkle with chopped nuts, if desired. Freeze until solid, about 1 hour.

3 Slice and serve, or keep frozen until ready to use. Allow to thaw 5 to 10 minutes for easier slicing.

To soften the ice cream, break it up in a bowl and stir with a wooden spoon. But beware...don't let the ice cream reach the melting point, or when you refreeze it, it will crystallize.

Raspberry Chiffon Pie

Serves 8

1 cup heavy cream

1 (8-ounce) package cream cheese, softened

1 (10-ounce) jar raspberry preserves

1 (9-inch) graham cracker pie crust

Fresh raspberries and mint leaves for garnish (optional)

1 In a medium bowl with an electric mixer on medium-high speed, beat whipping cream until stiff peaks form; set aside.

2 In a large bowl, beat cream cheese on medium-high speed until smooth. Add raspberry preserves. Beat on low just until combined. Gently fold in whipped cream. Spoon mixture into pie crust.

3 Cover and freeze at least 4 hours, or until firm. Garnish with fresh raspberries and mint leaves, if desired.

When fresh raspberries are in season and a bargain at the market, add some to the cream cheese mixture to freshen up the flavor!

Dutch Apple Crumb Pie

Serves 8

1 refrigerated rolled pie crust (from a 15-ounce package)

1-¼ cups plus 1 tablespoon all-purpose flour, divided

⅓ cup quick-cooking oats

½ cup light brown sugar

2-¼ teaspoons cinnamon, divided

¼ teaspoon salt

1 stick butter, softened

2 pounds Granny Smith apples, peeled, cored, thinly sliced

½ cup granulated sugar

Confectioners' sugar for dusting

1 Preheat oven to 350 degrees F. Unroll pie crust and place in a 9-inch deep dish pie plate, pressing crust firmly into plate; flute edges and set aside.

2 In a large bowl, combine 1-¼ cups flour, oats, brown sugar, 2 teaspoons cinnamon, and salt. Using a knife in scissor-like fashion, cut in butter, creating large crumbs.

3 In another large bowl, toss apples with granulated sugar, remaining flour, and remaining cinnamon. Spoon apple mixture into pie crust. Sprinkle crumb mixture over apples, packing lightly. Place pie on baking sheet.

4 Bake 1-¼ hours, or until apples are tender and crumbs are golden. If crumbs become too brown, place a 4-inch square of foil over middle of pie for remaining baking time. Cool on wire rack. Dust with confectioners' sugar before serving.

Team Member Favorite:
Every Thanksgiving, Jodi, our Project Coordinator, makes this pie as the crowning point to her festive meal. And luckily, she shared this recipe so it can now be a part of your holiday festivities.

Pink Lemonade Pie

Serves 8

1 (8-ounce) package cream cheese, softened

1 (6-ounce) container frozen pink lemonade concentrate, thawed

1 (8-ounce) container frozen whipped topping, thawed

4 drops red food color (optional)

1 (9-inch) prepared shortbread pie crust

1 In a medium bowl, beat cream cheese until smooth. Add lemonade concentrate and beat until well combined. Fold in whipped topping and food color, if desired.

2 Spoon into pie crust.

3 Freeze 20 minutes. Serve, or cover and chill until ready to serve.

Serving Suggestion:
Pink Lemonade Pie tastes great frozen, too. If you want to keep it in the freezer, just remove it about 5 minutes before serving, and garnish with dollops of whipped cream and lemon slices.

Nutty Buddy Pie

Makes 8

1 refrigerated rolled pie crust (from a 15-ounce package)

4 eggs

1-¼ cups light corn syrup

¾ cup sugar

½ stick butter, melted

1 teaspoon vanilla extract

⅛ teaspoon salt

1-¼ cups salted peanuts

½ cup mini chocolate chips

French vanilla ice cream (optional)

1 Preheat oven to 350 degrees F. Unroll pie crust and place in a 9-inch pie plate, pressing crust firmly into plate; set aside.

2 In a large bowl, beat eggs. Whisk in corn syrup, sugar, butter, vanilla, and salt. Stir in peanuts and chocolate chips. Pour filling into pie crust. To prevent overbrowning, cover pie edge with foil.

3 Bake 25 minutes. Remove foil and bake 35 to 40 additional minutes, or until center is set. Cool on a wire rack. Cover and refrigerate until ready to serve. Serve with ice cream, if desired.

About this Recipe:
Patty, our Test Kitchen Director, loved those ice cream cone sundaes while growing up. Well, that was the inspiration for this pie. Thanks, Patty!!

Toasty S'mores Pie

Serves 8

2 cups graham cracker crumbs

¼ cup sugar

1-½ sticks butter, melted

2 (4-serving-size) packages instant chocolate pudding and pie filling

3 cups milk

1 cup frozen whipped topping, thawed

2 cups mini marshmallows

1 Preheat oven to 350 degrees F. In a medium bowl, combine graham cracker crumbs, sugar, and melted butter. Reserve ¼ cup of the mixture and press the remaining crumbs into a 9-inch, deep dish pie plate. Bake 8 minutes.

2 In a large bowl, whisk the pudding mix and milk 1 to 2 minutes, or until thickened. Fold in whipped topping to combine.

3 Set the oven to broil. Spoon pudding mixture into the crust. Sprinkle remaining graham cracker crumbs on top of pudding. Cover completely with marshmallows.

4 Place under broiler 1 to 2 minutes, or until marshmallows are golden. (Leave the door cracked a bit to watch them; make sure they don't burn!) Remove pie from oven, let cool 10 minutes, before refrigerating 2 hours, or until ready to serve.

Frozen Grasshopper Pie

Serves 8

1 (4.67-ounce) package thin chocolate-covered mint candies, divided

1 quart vanilla ice cream, softened

2 teaspoons crème de menthe liqueur (see Tip)

teaspoon green food color

1 (9-inch) chocolate graham cracker pie crust

1 Reserve 8 candies; chop remaining candies and place in a large bowl.

2 Add ice cream, crème de menthe, and food color; mix well then spoon into pie crust.

3 Garnish with the reserved candies around the pie by pressing each halfway into the ice cream. Freeze at least 4 hours, or until firm. Cut into slices and serve.

If you'd prefer to make this without the liqueur, you can substitute 1 teaspoon mint extract for the crème de menthe to get the desired minty flavor. And, for extra richness, garnish with whipped cream. Mmm!

Prize-Winning Pie Crust

Makes 2 (9-inch) pie crusts

¾ cup plus 2 tablespoons all-vegetable shortening

6 tablespoons boiling water

2 teaspoons milk

2-¼ cups all-purpose flour

1 teaspoon salt

1 In a medium bowl, whisk shortening, water, and milk until it reaches the consistency of whipped cream. Add flour and salt; stir well with a spoon until dough forms a ball. Divide dough into 2 equal-sized balls.

2 Place 1 dough ball between 2 sheets of wax paper; with a rolling pin, roll out to a circle slightly larger than a 9-inch pie plate. Place in bottom of a 9-inch pie plate.

To use as an unbaked shell: Fill with desired pie filling and bake according to filling directions.

To use as a baked shell: Prick surface of dough with a fork several times and bake in a preheated 425 degree oven 12 to 15 minutes; cool and fill as desired.

To use top crust: After filling bottom crust, but before baking, roll out second dough ball to the same size and place over filling; seal by pinching edges together. Trim excess dough. Using a paring knife, cut 6 slits to allow steam to escape while baking. Bake according to filling directions, or until crust is golden.

Did You Know?

If you only need one pie crust, wrap the second crust in plastic and refrigerate. It will keep for several days in the fridge, or it can be frozen until ready to use.

No-Roll Pie Crust

Makes 1 (9-inch) Pie Crust

1-½ cups all-purpose flour

2 tablespoons sugar

1 teaspoon salt

½ cup vegetable oil

2 tablespoons cold milk

1 Sift flour, sugar, and salt into a 9-inch pie plate. In a 1-cup measuring cup, whisk together oil and milk and pour over flour mixture.

2 Using a fork, mix until completely dampened. Press dough evenly over bottom of pie plate then up sides and over rim.

To use as an unbaked shell: Fill with desired pie filling and bake according to filling directions.

To use as a baked shell: Prick surface of dough with a fork several times and bake in a preheated 425 degree oven 12 to 15 minutes; cool and fill as desired.

Test Kitchen Mr. Food Hints & Tips

Patty shows off her easy-as-can-be pie crust to Howard in the Test Kitchen. She went on to share with him that this crust is more like a buttery shortbread than a traditional pie crust.

Cheesecakes

Strawberry Swirl Cheesecake

Serves 12

2 cups graham cracker crumbs

1 stick butter, melted

1-¼ cups plus 2 tablespoons sugar, divided

3 (8-ounce) packages cream cheese, softened

4 eggs

2 teaspoons vanilla extract, divided

4 tablespoons seedless strawberry jam, divided

6 drops red food color, divided

1 (16-ounce) container sour cream

1 (10-ounce) package frozen strawberry halves in syrup, thawed

1 Preheat oven to 350 degrees F. In a medium bowl, combine graham cracker crumbs, butter, and 2 tablespoons sugar; mix well then spread mixture into bottom and halfway up sides of a 10-inch springform pan. Chill until ready to fill.

2 In a large bowl with an electric mixer on medium speed, blend cream cheese and 1 cup sugar. Add eggs, one at a time, blending after each addition. Add 1 teaspoon vanilla; mix well. Reserve ½ cup of filling in a small bowl. Pour remaining filling over chilled crust.

3 Add 2 tablespoons strawberry jam and 3 drops red food color to reserved filling; mix well. Drop spoonfuls onto cheesecake filling, then run a knife in a swirl pattern through cheesecake. Bake 55 to 60 minutes, or until firm. Remove from oven and let sit 5 minutes.

4 Meanwhile, in a medium bowl, mix sour cream, remaining sugar, and remaining vanilla with a spoon until well combined. Pour 1-½ cups of sour cream mixture over top of cheesecake. Mix remaining sour cream mixture with remaining strawberry jam and food color. Drizzle over top and swirl with a knife. Bake 5 additional minutes. Remove from oven and let cool completely at room temperature.

5 Refrigerate overnight. Remove from pan, slice, and drizzle with strawberries in syrup.

Guilt-Free Cannoli Cheesecake

Serves 8

- 1 cup graham cracker crumbs
- ¼ cup chopped almonds
- 3 tablespoons butter, melted
- 1 (15-ounce) container part-skim ricotta cheese
- 1 cup plain low-fat yogurt
- ¾ cup sugar
- 2 tablespoons all-purpose flour
- 1 teaspoon almond extract
- 1 teaspoon orange zest
- 1 (8-ounce) package reduced-fat cream cheese, softened
- 2 eggs
- 1 teaspoon vanilla extract
- ½ cup mini chocolate chips

1 Preheat oven to 350 degrees F. In a small bowl, combine graham cracker crumbs, almonds, and butter; press into bottom and up sides of a 9-inch deep-dish pie plate.

2 Bake 3 to 5 minutes, or until lightly browned; let cool. (Leave the oven on.)

3 In a large bowl with an electric mixer on medium speed, combine ricotta cheese, yogurt, sugar, flour, almond extract, and orange zest until well combined; set aside.

4 In another large bowl with an electric mixer on medium speed, beat cream cheese, eggs, and vanilla until thoroughly combined. Stir in ricotta mixture and chocolate chips until well combined. Pour into pie crust.

5 Bake 60 to 65 minutes, or until center is nearly set. Cool 30 to 45 minutes, then refrigerate overnight before serving.

Crispy Cheesecake Squares

Makes 18

1 (8- to 9-inch) frozen cheesecake, slightly thawed

2 cups frozen strawberries

1 cup frozen blueberries

¼ cup plus 2 tablespoons sugar, divided

2-½ cups oven-toasted corn cereal, coarsely crushed

1 teaspoon ground cinnamon

1 tablespoon butter, melted

½ cup light corn syrup

¼ teaspoon vanilla extract

1 Cut cheesecake into 1-½-inch squares, place on platter, cover, and return to freezer.

2 In a medium saucepan, combine strawberries, blueberries, and ¼ cup sugar. Cook over medium-high heat 15 minutes, or until fruit breaks down and sauce has thickened, stirring occasionally. Let cool and refrigerate until chilled.

3 Meanwhile, in a shallow dish, combine cereal, remaining sugar, cinnamon, and butter; mix well.

4 In a small bowl, combine corn syrup and vanilla. Drizzle a teaspoon of corn syrup mixture over each cheesecake square, one at a time, then place in cereal mixture dish. Sprinkle cereal mixture over cheesecake square until all sides are coated evenly. Place on platter. Repeat with remaining squares.

5 Cover and freeze until ready to serve or serve immediately with berry sauce drizzled over the top of each piece.

Team Member Favorite:
Jaime, one of our Test Kitchen Team Members, and a busy mom, loves using shortcuts like this when her family comes together.

Blueberry Cheesecake Parfaits

Serves 10

- 2 (8-ounce) packages cream cheese, softened
- ⅓ cup confectioners' sugar
- 1 cup sour cream
- 1-½ cups frozen whipped topping, thawed
- 10 vanilla wafers
- 7 cups blueberries (about 3-½ pints)
- 1 tablespoon orange-flavored liqueur (optional)

1 In a large bowl, mix together the cream cheese, confectioners' sugar, and sour cream until smooth. Fold whipped topping into the cream cheese mixture.

2 Put a vanilla wafer in the bottom of each of ten glasses.

3 Toss the blueberries in orange-flavored liqueur, if desired. Fill glasses about two-thirds full with berries. Add 3 tablespoons of cream cheese mixture to each glass and lightly shake it down so it oozes over the berries. Add another tablespoon of berries to each glass, another tablespoon of cream cheese mixture, and top with a few berries.

4 Serve immediately or refrigerate 1 to 2 hours before serving.

Chocolate Hazelnut Cheesecake

Serves 16

2 cups graham cracker crumbs

1 stick butter, melted

2 (8-ounce) packages cream cheese, softened

¾ cup confectioners' sugar

1 (13-ounce) jar chocolate hazelnut spread (like Nutella)

½ cup heavy cream

8 chocolate-covered hazelnut candies, chopped

1 In a medium bowl, combine graham cracker crumbs and butter; mix well then spread mixture into bottom and halfway up sides of a 9-inch springform pan. Chill until ready to fill.

2 In a large bowl with an electric mixer on medium speed, blend cream cheese and confectioners' sugar until smooth. Add in chocolate hazelnut spread; mix well. Add heavy cream and beat until it has a mousse-like texture. Stir hazelnut candies into mixture.

3 Pour mixture over crust, and refrigerate at least 8 hours or overnight.

Serving Suggestion:

When ready to serve, why not dollop each slice with whipped cream and garnish with half a hazelnut candy? We like to use Ferrero Rocher candies, but as always...any brand will do.

Cookies 'n' Cream Cheesecake

Serves 12

1 (20-ounce) package cream-filled chocolate sandwich cookies, divided

¾ stick butter, melted

3 (8-ounce) packages cream cheese, softened

1-¼ cups sugar, divided

4 eggs

2 teaspoons vanilla extract, divided

1 (16-ounce) container sour cream

1 tablespoon unsweetened cocoa powder

Whipped cream for garnish

1 Preheat oven to 350 degrees F. Place 30 cookies in a resealable plastic bag; using a rolling pin, crush cookies. Place crumbs in a medium bowl with the butter; mix well then spread mixture into bottom and halfway up sides of a 10-inch springform pan. Chill until ready to use.

2 In a large bowl with an electric mixer on medium speed, beat cream cheese and 1 cup sugar until creamy. Add eggs one at a time, beating well after each addition, then add 1 teaspoon vanilla and mix well. Set aside 6 cookies for garnish then coarsely break up remaining cookies. Stir cookie pieces into cream cheese mixture then pour into crust.

3 Bake 55 to 60 minutes, or until firm. Remove from oven and let cool 5 minutes.

4 Meanwhile, in a medium bowl, using a spoon, stir together sour cream, cocoa, remaining sugar, and remaining vanilla until well combined. Carefully spread sour cream mixture over top of cheesecake then bake 5 additional minutes.

5 Let cool completely at room temperature, then chill 8 hours or overnight. Cover until ready to serve. When ready to serve, remove from pan to a serving plate, slice and garnish with whipped cream. Cut the 6 reserved cookies in half and place half a cookie on each slice.

Really Easy Ricotta Cheesecake

Serves 8

1 cup graham cracker crumbs

3 tablespoons butter, melted

1 (15-ounce) container ricotta cheese

1 (8-ounce) package cream cheese, softened

1 cup sugar

2 tablespoons all-purpose flour

2 eggs

1 teaspoon vanilla extract

2 tablespoons lemon juice

Zest of 1 orange

Zest of 1 lime

1 Preheat oven to 350 degree F.

2 In a small bowl, combine graham cracker crumbs and butter; press into bottom and up sides of a 9-inch deep-dish pie plate.

3 Bake 3 to 5 minutes, or until lightly browned; let cool. (Leave the oven on.)

4 In a large bowl with an electric mixer on medium speed, combine ricotta cheese, cream cheese, sugar, and flour; mix well. Beat in eggs, vanilla, and lemon juice until smooth. Stir in orange and lime zests. Pour into pie crust.

5 Bake 50 to 60 minutes, or until center is nearly set. Cool 45 minutes, then refrigerate 8 hours or overnight before serving.

To prevent cheesecake from cracking there are a couple of easy simple tips...first, don't over mix it. Next, let it cool slowly at room temperature before refrigerating. Easy enough, huh?

Toffee Cheesecake Pie

Serves 8

- 1 (16.5-ounce) roll refrigerated chocolate chip cookie dough
- 2 (8-ounce) packages cream cheese, softened
- 2 eggs
- ½ cup sugar
- 1 teaspoon vanilla extract
- 4 (1.4-ounce) toffee candy bars, coarsely chopped (like Skor or Heath)

1. Preheat oven to 350 degrees F. Coat a 9-inch deep dish pie plate with cooking spray.

2. Slice cookie dough into 24 slices and arrange on bottom and up sides of prepared pie plate. Press dough together, making a uniform crust; set aside.

3. In a large bowl with an electric mixer on medium speed, beat cream cheese, eggs, sugar, and vanilla 1 minute, or until well mixed. Stir in candy pieces and pour into pie plate.

4. Bake 40 to 45 minutes, or until center is firm. Remove from oven and allow to cool completely at room temperature. Cover loosely, then chill at least 4 hours before serving.

Fresh Fruit Cheesecake Tarts

Makes 6

1 (8-ounce) package cream cheese, softened

2 tablespoons orange marmalade

⅓ cup sugar

6 single-serving graham cracker tart shells

1-½ cups assorted fresh berries or other fruit, cut into bite-sized pieces, if necessary

1 In a medium bowl with an electric mixer on medium speed, beat cream cheese, marmalade, and sugar 2 minutes, or until well combined.

2 Spoon mixture evenly into tart shells, then top with equal amounts of fruit. Loosely cover and chill at least 2 hours before serving.

Lighten It Up:
Trying to cut back a bit but still want big flavor? No problem, Simply use reduced-fat cream cheese, and sugar-free orange marmalade instead of their regular counterparts.

Classic New York Cheesecake

Serves 12

- 1 (16.5-ounce) roll refrigerated sugar cookie dough, cut into ½-inch slices
- 4 (8-ounce) packages cream cheese, softened
- 1-¼ cups sugar
- 2 eggs
- ½ cup sour cream
- ¾ cup all-purpose flour
- 1 teaspoon vanilla extract
- 2 tablespoons lemon juice

1 Preheat oven to 400 degrees F. Coat bottom of a 9-inch springform pan with cooking spray.

2 Line bottom of prepared pan with half the cookie dough slices; with your fingers, spread dough to create a solid crust. Bake 10 minutes, or until golden. Let cool.

3 Press remaining dough slices around sides of pan to create a side crust; set aside. Increase oven temperature to 475 degrees.

4 In a large bowl, beat cream cheese with sugar until smooth. Beat in remaining ingredients until well combined. Spoon batter into crust and bake 12 to 15 minutes, or until top is golden. Reduce oven temperature to 350 degrees and bake 30 additional minutes.

5 Remove cheesecake from oven; let cool completely at room temperature. Remove springform pan ring; cover and chill at least 6 hours before serving.

Did You Know?

Years ago, the Mr. Food Test Kitchen Team scoured New York City looking for the best deli-style cheesecake. We found it at the Carnegie Deli. Now we're sharing our easy at-home version with you.

Key Lime Pie Cheesecake

Serves 8

1 (8 ounce) package cream cheese, softened

1 (14 ounce) can sweetened condensed milk

1 (12 ounce) container frozen whipped topping, thawed

1 cup Key lime or lime juice (see Tip)

1 baked 9-inch pie shell

Lime slices and fresh mint leaves for garnish (optional)

1 In a large bowl, combine cream cheese, sweetened condensed milk, and whipped topping. Stir in lime juice until well blended and mixture is thick and smooth.

2 Immediately pour lime filling into pie shell. Chill for about 4 hours.

3 Garnish with fresh lime slices and fresh mint leaves, if desired.

Did you know there is a difference between regular limes and Key limes? Key limes are smaller and have a tarter flavor. You can even find bottled Key lime juice in your market. Look for it, it really adds a very authentic flavor.

Cookies

Chocolate Walnut Chippers

Makes 60

1-½ sticks butter, softened

1-½ cups sugar

2 large eggs

1 cup all-purpose flour

¾ cup unsweetened cocoa powder

1 teaspoon baking powder

2 cups white chocolate chips

1 cup coarsely chopped walnuts

1 Preheat oven to 350 degrees F.

2 In a large bowl with an electric mixer on medium speed, beat butter and sugar until creamy. Add eggs, flour, cocoa, and baking powder, beating until blended. Stir in white chocolate chips and walnuts. Drop mixture by heaping teaspoonfuls onto ungreased baking sheets.

3 Bake 9 to 10 minutes, or until set around edges.

4 Cool cookies 1 minute on baking sheets, then remove to wire racks to cool completely. Store in an airtight container.

Make sure you leave an inch or so between the cookie dough when placing them on the baking sheets so there's room for these to spread during baking.

Java Coconut Drops

Makes 36

Cookies:

- 2 cups all-purpose flour
- ½ teaspoon salt
- ½ teaspoon baking soda
- 3 (1-ounce) squares unsweetened baking chocolate
- ¼ cup hot coffee
- 1 stick butter
- 1 cup firmly packed brown sugar
- 1 egg
- ½ cup sour cream
- ½ cup shredded coconut

Frosting:

- 1 (1-ounce) square unsweetened baking chocolate
- 1 tablespoon butter
- 2 tablespoons sour cream
- 1 cup confectioners' sugar

1 Preheat oven to 375 degrees F. Coat baking sheets with cooking spray. In a small bowl, combine flour, salt, and baking soda; set aside.

2 In a small saucepan, melt 3 squares of chocolate in coffee over low heat; set aside to cool.

3 In a large bowl, cream together 1 stick butter and brown sugar. Add egg and cooled chocolate mixture and beat well. Add sour cream and flour mixture alternately, mixing well. Add coconut and mix well. Drop by heaping teaspoonfuls onto prepared baking sheets. Bake 12 to 15 minutes, or until firm to touch.

4 Meanwhile, to make chocolate frosting, in a small microwaveable bowl, microwave 1 square baking chocolate, 1 tablespoon butter, and 2 tablespoons sour cream on low power. Mix well, then slowly blend in confectioners' sugar and mix again. Frost cookies while warm. Let cool then store in an airtight container.

We found that if the batter seems a bit too thick, add a few drops of milk or water until it's the consistency of cookie dough.

Almond Florentine Cookies

Makes 15 sandwich cookies

¾ cup sugar

¼ cup all-purpose flour

2-½ cups sliced almonds

1 egg white, lightly beaten

5 tablespoons butter, melted

1 teaspoon vanilla extract

1-½ cups semisweet chocolate chips

1 Preheat oven to 350 degrees F. Line baking sheets with parchment paper (see Tip).

2 In a large bowl, stir together sugar, flour, and almonds; stir in egg white, butter, and vanilla until blended. Drop 30 rounded tablespoonfuls of dough onto prepared baking sheets, about 2 inches apart.

3 Bake 10 to 12 minutes, or until golden. Cool on baking sheets.

4 When cookies are cool, in a microwaveable bowl, melt chocolate chips in the microwave. Spoon a small amount of chocolate on half the cookies. Spread almost to edges, and top with other cookies. Press down slightly. Store in an airtight container.

For most cookies, don't worry about lining the baking sheet with parchment paper, but in this case, it will help in removing the delicate almond cookies from the pan after baking. You can usually find parchment paper near aluminum foil in the market.

Lemonade Cookies

Makes 48

2 sticks butter, softened

1 cup plus 2 tablespoons sugar, divided

2 eggs

3 cups all-purpose flour

1 teaspoon baking soda

1 (6-ounce) can frozen lemonade concentrate, thawed, divided

1 tablespoon lemon zest

1 Preheat oven to 400 degrees F.

2 In a large bowl, cream together butter and 1 cup sugar. Add eggs, beating well. In another large bowl, combine flour and baking soda and add alternately with ½ cup of lemonade concentrate into egg mixture. Stir in lemon zest. Drop by teaspoonfuls 2 inches apart onto ungreased baking sheets.

3 Bake 8 to 9 minutes, or until edges are light brown.

4 Remove from oven and brush hot cookies lightly with remaining lemonade concentrate. Sprinkle cookies with remaining sugar. Let cool then store in an airtight container.

Fresh lemon zest adds a real burst of flavor to these cookies. Just don't use any of the white part, or pith, as it is very bitter.

Chocolate Mint Sandwich Cookies

Makes 24 sandwich cookies

Chocolate Wafers:

1-¼ cups all-purpose flour

½ cup unsweetened cocoa powder

1 teaspoon baking soda

¼ teaspoon baking powder

¼ teaspoon salt

1 cup granulated sugar

1 stick butter, softened

1 egg

Mint Cream Filling:

½ stick butter, softened

2 ounces cream cheese, softened

2 cups confectioners' sugar

1 teaspoon mint extract

2-3 drops green food color

1 Preheat oven to 375 degrees F.

2 In a large bowl with an electric mixer, make chocolate wafers by mixing together flour, cocoa powder, baking soda, baking powder, salt, and sugar. Beat in 1 stick butter and egg until dough comes together. Drop 48 rounded teaspoons of dough onto ungreased baking sheets, about 2 inches apart. Slightly flatten dough with fingers.

3 Bake 9 to 11 minutes, or until cookies look set. Let cool.

4 In a medium bowl, make cream filling by combining ½ stick butter and cream cheese. Gradually beat in confectioners' sugar, mint extract, and food color until filling is fluffy. Place a teaspoon of filling onto center of one chocolate wafer and lightly press another chocolate wafer on top until cream comes to edge. Repeat with remaining wafers. Serve or keep refrigerated until ready to serve.

Anytime Wedding Cookies

Makes 60

2 sticks butter, softened

⅓ cup granulated sugar

2 teaspoons vanilla extract

2 teaspoons water

2 cups all-purpose flour

1 cup finely chopped pecans

½ cup confectioners' sugar

1 Preheat oven to 325 degrees F.

2 In a large bowl, with an electric mixer, cream butter and granulated sugar until fluffy. Add vanilla and water; beat well. With a spoon, stir in flour and pecans. Shape into 1-inch balls and place about 1 inch apart on ungreased baking sheets.

3 Bake 20 to 25 minutes, or until bottoms of cookies are light golden. Remove to wire racks to cool completely.

4 Place confectioners' sugar in a resealable plastic bag; add a few cookies at a time and shake until completely coated. Store in an airtight container until ready to serve.

Serving Suggestion:
We don't need to just serve these at weddings, so keep 'em on hand for drop-in company, since they'll stay fresh for a couple of weeks if stored properly.

Iced Carrot Cake Cookies

Makes 60

1 (18-ounce) package carrot cake mix

1 (8-ounce) can crushed pineapple, drained

2 carrots, finely shredded

2 eggs

2 tablespoons vegetable oil

1 cup chopped pecans

1 (16-ounce) container cream cheese frosting

1 Preheat oven to 350 degrees F. Coat baking sheets with cooking spray.

2 In a large bowl, combine cake mix, pineapple, carrots, eggs, and oil; beat 3 to 4 minutes, or until well blended. Stir in pecans. Drop by teaspoonfuls 1 inch apart onto prepared baking sheets.

3 Bake 14 to 16 minutes, or until edges are golden. Remove to a wire rack to cool, then frost with cream cheese frosting. Store in an airtight container.

Good for You!

These aren't exactly a health food but they are loaded with beta-carotene which may help improve our vision and assist with slowing down our aging process. Guess that proves that if you eat these for 100 years, you'll live a long life. (Ha ha!)

Southern Pecan Sandies

Makes 48

2 sticks butter, softened

¼ cup confectioners' sugar

2 teaspoons vanilla extract

2 cups all-purpose flour

1 cup chopped pecans

1 Preheat oven to 325 degree F.

2 In a large bowl with an electric mixer on medium speed, cream butter and confectioners' sugar 1 minute. Add vanilla; mix well. With a spoon, stir in flour and pecans. Drop by teaspoonfuls about 1 inch apart onto ungreased baking sheets.

3 Bake 12 to 15 minutes, or until edges are golden. (Do not overbake.)

4 Let cool and serve, or store in an airtight container.

Serving Suggestion:
Dust the tops of these with a bit of confectioners' sugar right before serving. Oh, and if ya serve 'em up with some sweet tea, it's Southern hospitality at its best.

Chinese Almond Rounds

Makes 36

¾ cup sugar, plus extra for sprinkling

1 teaspoon baking powder

1-½ sticks butter, softened

1 egg

2 tablespoons water

1 teaspoon almond extract

2-½ cups all-purpose flour

⅓ cup whole shelled almonds

1 Preheat oven to 350 degrees F. Coat baking sheets with cooking spray.

2 In a large bowl with an electric mixer on medium speed, combine ¾ cup sugar, baking powder, butter, egg, water, and almond extract; blend well. Gradually add flour, blending on low speed until well mixed.

3 Shape dough into 1-inch balls and place about 2 inches apart on prepared baking sheets. Flatten balls slightly with the bottom of a glass, then evenly sprinkle with sugar; press an almond firmly into center of each cookie.

4 Bake 8 to 12 minutes, or until firm to the touch but not brown. (Do not overbake.) Immediately remove from baking sheets and cool on wire racks. Store in an airtight container.

Buttery Cutout Cookies

Makes 36

2 sticks butter, softened

¾ cup sugar

2 eggs

1 teaspoon vanilla extract

3-½ cups all-purpose flour

1 In a large bowl with an electric mixer on medium speed, cream the butter and sugar. Add eggs and vanilla; beat 1 to 2 minutes, or until light and fluffy. Gradually add flour and beat 2 minutes, or until well blended. Form dough into 2 balls; cover and chill at least 2 hours.

2 Preheat oven to 350 degree F.

3 On a lightly floured work surface, using a rolling pin, roll 1 ball of dough to ¼-inch thickness. Using cookie cutters or a knife, cut into desired shapes. Place shapes 1 inch apart on ungreased baking sheets. Repeat with remaining ball of dough.

4 Bake 10 to 12 minutes, or until golden around the edges. Remove to a wire rack to cool completely, then decorate and store in an airtight container.

These can fit any occasion just by using different holiday or themed cookie cutters. Before baking, maybe sprinkle with colored sugar or sprinkles, or once they cool, feel free to frost and decorate them with homemade or store-bought icing tinted with a few drops of food color. You can even pipe the edges with an accenting color of store-bought piping gel to give them a really finished look.

Easiest Peanut Butter Cookies

Makes 30

1 cup peanut butter

1 cup sugar, plus extra for sprinkling

1 large egg

1 teaspoon vanilla extract

1 Preheat oven to 325 degrees F.

2 In a large bowl, stir together all ingredients until combined. Shape dough into 1-inch balls and place 1 inch apart on ungreased baking sheets. Flatten gently in a crisscross pattern with tines of a fork. Sprinkle with sugar.

3 Bake 15 minutes, or until golden. Remove to wire racks to cool, then store in an airtight container.

Good news! This dough freezes well, so you can shape these into balls and freeze 'em. Keep a batch on hand to bake whenever a craving for fresh baked cookies strikes.

Coconut Cherry Surprises

Makes 24

2 sticks butter

½ cup sugar

2 teaspoons vanilla extract

2 cups all-purpose flour

½ teaspoon salt

2 dozen maraschino cherries, drained and dried

1 cup shredded coconut

1 Preheat oven to 350 degrees F. Coat baking sheets with cooking spray.

2 In a large bowl, cream together butter, sugar, and vanilla. Stir in flour and salt.

3 Form dough into 1-inch balls. Make an indentation with your finger, then press a cherry into the center of each. Reshape each into a ball, completely covering cherries. Roll balls in shredded coconut and place 2 inches apart on prepared baking sheets.

4 Bake 17 to 20 minutes, or until firm, then cool on wire racks. Store in an airtight container.

About This Recipe:

Patty, our Test Kitchen Director suggests substituting dates, almonds, or walnuts for the cherries and surprise your gang every time you make these.

Kelly's Ricotta Cookies

Makes 30

½ cup ricotta cheese

1 stick butter

1 teaspoon vanilla extract

1 egg

2 cups all-purpose flour

1 cup granulated sugar

½ teaspoon baking soda

½ teaspoon salt

Confectioners' sugar for dusting

1 Preheat oven to 375 degrees F.

2 In a large bowl, combine ricotta cheese, butter, and vanilla. Beat in egg; mix well. Stir in flour, sugar, baking soda, and salt until well combined. Drop by teaspoonfuls 1 inch apart, onto ungreased baking sheets.

3 Bake 10 to 12 minutes, or until light brown around edges. Let cool, then dust with confectioners' sugar. Store in an airtight container.

About This Recipe:

Kelly, from our Test Kitchen, loves when her Mom makes these dusted with confectioners' sugar, but you can top them with a quick icing, by mixing together 1 cup confectioners' sugar, 1 tablespoon milk, 1 teaspoon lemon juice and 1 to 2 drops yellow food color for that extra-fancy look.

Potato Chip Cookies

Makes 48

4 sticks butter, softened

1 cup sugar

3-¼ cups all-purpose flour

1 teaspoon vanilla extract

1-½ cups coarsely crushed
potato chips

1 Preheat oven to 300 degrees F.

2 In a large bowl, cream butter and sugar. Slowly add flour and vanilla until well blended. Stir in potato chips; mix well.

3 Drop by rounded teaspoonfuls 2 inches apart onto ungreased baking sheets. Using a fork, flatten each cookie.

4 Bake 20 to 22 minutes, or until light golden around edges. Let stand 5 minutes, then remove to a wire rack to cool completely. Store in an airtight container.

After they're cool, we suggest sprinkling these with confectioners' sugar or better yet, drizzle 'em with melted chocolate. To easily melt the chocolate, place ½ cup semisweet chocolate chips and 1 teaspoon vegetable shortening in a small microwaveable bowl, and microwave it for 45 to 60 seconds until melted and smooth when stirred together. Then, drizzle it on with a fork and watch these cookies disappear.

Maui Chocolate Chip Cookies

Makes 24

1 stick butter, melted

1 egg

1 teaspoon vanilla extract

¾ cup sugar

1-¼ cups all-purpose flour

½ teaspoon baking soda

½ teaspoon salt

½ cup coarsely chopped macadamia nuts

1 cup semisweet chocolate chips

1 Preheat oven to 375 degrees F. Coat baking sheets with cooking spray.

2 In a large bowl, combine butter, egg, vanilla, and sugar; mix well. Stir in flour, baking soda, and salt. Add nuts and chocolate chips; mix well. Drop heaping tablespoonfuls onto prepared baking sheets about 2 inches apart.

3 Bake 10 to 12 minutes, or until edges are brown. Let cool 5 minutes and remove to a wire rack to cool completely. Store in an airtight container.

Serving suggestion:

Why not make these into mini ice cream sandwiches by topping the flat side of half the cookies with a scoop of vanilla ice cream and sandwiching them with another cookie? Then wrap them up and keep them in the freezer for a quick treat that your gang will love.

Almond Chocolate Macaroons

Makes 36

1 cup (6 ounces) semisweet chocolate chips

1 cup shredded coconut

½ cup finely chopped almonds

2 egg whites

¼ teaspoon salt

½ cup sugar

½ teaspoon almond extract

1 In a large saucepan, melt chocolate over low heat. Let cool 5 to 10 minutes. Stir in coconut and almonds.

2 Preheat oven to 350 degrees F. Line baking sheets with aluminum foil.

3 In a medium bowl with an electric mixer on high speed, beat egg whites and salt until foamy. Gradually add sugar, 1 tablespoon at a time, beating until stiff peaks form and sugar dissolves (2 to 4 minutes). Add almond extract, then fold egg white mixture into chocolate mixture. Drop by rounded teaspoonfuls onto prepared baking sheets.

4 Bake 10 minutes. Cool 1 minute on baking sheets; transfer cookies to wire racks to cool completely. Store in an airtight container.

Good for You!

Since almonds are high in monounsaturated fats, which are the same type of health-promoting fats that are found in olive oil and which have been associated with reducing the risk of heart disease, we can feel good about adding them in.

Grandma's Spice Cookies

Makes 48

1 (18.25-ounce) package spice cake mix

2 sticks butter, softened

2 eggs

1 cup crushed cornflakes

1 cup quick-cooking oats

1 cup shredded coconut

1 cup chopped walnuts

1 cup raisins

2 tablespoons sugar

1 Preheat oven to 350 degrees F.

2 In a large bowl, combine cake mix, butter, and eggs; mix well. Add cornflakes, oats, coconut, walnuts, and raisins; mix well.

3 Drop dough by rounded teaspoonfuls 2 inches apart onto ungreased baking sheets. Flatten them with bottom of a glass that's frequently dipped in sugar.

4 Bake 12 minutes, or until set. Cool 5 minutes, then remove from baking sheets and let cool completely. Store in an airtight container.

Did You Know:

The easiest way to crush the cornflakes is to put them in a resealable plastic bag, seal it, and roll a can from your pantry over it a few times.

Jam-Filled Split Seconds

Makes 30

1-½ sticks butter, softened

⅔ cup sugar

1 egg

2 teaspoons vanilla extract

2 cups all-purpose flour

½ teaspoon baking powder

⅓ cup strawberry, raspberry, or apricot jam

1 Preheat oven to 350 degrees F.

2 In a large bowl, combine butter, sugar, egg, and vanilla. With an electric mixer on low speed, blend in flour and baking powder; mix well.

3 Place dough on a lightly floured surface and divide into 4 equal parts. Shape each part into a roll approximately 12 inches long and ¾ inches thick.

4 Place rolls on an ungreased baking sheet about 4 inches apart and 2 inches from edge of the pan. Using a wooden spoon handle, make a lengthwise depression in center of each roll, about ¼-inch to ⅓-inch deep, lengthwise. Fill depressions with jam.

5 Bake 15 to 20 minutes, or until golden. While still warm, cut diagonally into ¾-inch slices. Store in an airtight container.

Test Kitchen
Mr. Food
Hints & Tips

You can use your finger or a knife handle to make the depressions in the dough if you can't find your wooden spoon buried in your drawer.

White Chocolate Cranberry Biscotti

Makes 42

3 cups all-purpose flour

2 cups sugar

½ teaspoon salt

1 teaspoon baking powder

4 eggs

1 teaspoon vanilla extract

1 cup white chocolate chips

1 cup dried cranberries

1 Preheat oven to 350 degrees F. Coat two baking sheets with cooking spray.

2 In a large bowl, combine all ingredients except chocolate chips and cranberries; mix well. Using your hands, work dough until it forms a ball. Work in white chocolate chips and cranberries until well combined. Place half the dough on one baking sheet and form into a 3- x 12-inch loaf about 1 inch high. Repeat with remaining dough on second baking sheet.

3 Bake 25 to 30 minutes, or until firm and light golden. Remove from oven and reduce heat to 325 degrees. Allow loaves to cool 5 minutes. Cut into ½-inch slices, and place cut-side down on baking sheets.

4 Bake 15 minutes then turn cookies over and bake 15 additional minutes, or until very crisp. Allow to cool, then serve, or store in an airtight container.

Candy Bar Cookies

Makes 36

1 (18.5-ounce) package white cake mix

⅓ cup vegetable oil

2 eggs

1 cup chopped candy bars (see Tip)

1 Preheat oven to 350 degrees F. Coat baking sheets with cooking spray.

2 In a large bowl, beat cake mix, oil, and eggs until well mixed. Stir in chopped candy bars. Drop by teaspoonfuls 2 inches apart onto prepared baking sheets.

3 Bake 7 to 10 minutes, or until golden. Cool cookies on a wire rack, then store in an airtight container.

Our Test Kitchen tried these lots of different candy bars, and our favorites were Snickers and Butterfinger. What will yours be? Let us know on Facebook.

Millie's Oatmeal Raisin Cookies

Makes 30

2 sticks butter, softened

1 cup granulated sugar

½ cup packed light brown sugar

2 eggs

1 teaspoon vanilla extract

2 cups all-purpose flour

1 teaspoon baking soda

1 teaspoon salt

1-½ cups quick-cooking oats

1-¼ cups raisins

1 Preheat oven to 375 degrees F. Coat baking sheets with cooking spray.

2 In a large bowl, cream together butter, granulated sugar, brown sugar, eggs, and vanilla. Add flour, baking soda, salt, and oats; mix well. Stir in raisins. Drop by tablespoonfuls onto prepared baking sheets.

3 Bake 10 to 12 minutes, or until lightly browned. Cool 3 to 5 minutes, then remove to wire racks to cool completely. Store in an airtight container.

Did You Know?
Millie is a dear friend of ours and she makes the best cookies ever. Trust us on this one. She told us, for a change of pace she uses both golden and regular raisins just to mix things up.

Peanut Cornflake Cookies

Makes 36

1 cup sugar

1 cup corn syrup

1 (18-ounce) jar peanut butter

6 cups cornflakes

¼ cup chopped peanuts

½ cup semi-sweet chocolate chips

1 Line baking sheets with parchment or wax paper.

2 In a medium saucepan over medium-high heat, combine sugar and corn syrup; stir until mixture comes to a full boil. Remove from heat and stir in peanut butter; mix well.

3 In a large bowl, combine cornflakes and peanuts. Add peanut butter mixture and mix well until evenly coated.

4 Using a tablespoon, form dough into 1-inch balls, and place them on prepared baking sheets.

5 Place chocolate in a microwaveable bowl and melt in the microwave 30 to 60 seconds, stirring until smooth. Drizzle melted chocolate over cookies. Let cool until chocolate is set. Serve or store in an airtight container.

Giant Chocolate Chip Cookies

Makes 13

2-¼ cups all-purpose flour

1 teaspoon baking soda

1 teaspoon salt

2 sticks butter, softened

¾ cup granulated sugar

¾ cup packed brown sugar

1 teaspoon vanilla extract

2 eggs

2 cups (12 ounces) semisweet
chocolate chips or chunks

1 Preheat oven to 375 degrees F.

2 In a small bowl, combine flour, baking soda, and salt; set aside. In a large bowl, beat butter, sugars, and vanilla until creamy. Beat in eggs. Gradually blend in flour mixture. Stir in chocolate chips. Form into 13 balls then place on ungreased baking sheets; flatten dough balls.

3 Bake 9 to 12 minutes, or until edges are brown. Let cool 5 minutes, then remove to wire racks to finish cooling. Store in an airtight container.

Did You Know?
The first record of chocolate chip cookies was in 1930 at the Tollhouse Inn in Massachusetts. Makes ya wonder what they dunked in their milk before that?

Apricot Peek-a-Boos

Makes 24 sandwich cookies

2 (18-ounce) rolls refrigerated
  sugar cookie dough

Confectioners' sugar for dusting

1 cup seedless apricot preserves

1 Freeze cookie dough 30 minutes. Preheat oven to 350 degrees F.

2 Remove one roll from freezer; cut into ¼-inch slices and place on ungreased baking sheets.

3 Bake 10 minutes, or until edges are golden. Remove from oven, let cool slightly then transfer to wire racks to cool completely.

4 Remove second roll from freezer; cut into ¼-inch slices and place on cooled baking sheets. Bake 10 minutes or until edges are golden. Immediately use a 1-inch cutter or a clean plastic bottle cap to cut out a round hole in center of this batch of cookies. Cool cookies on baking sheets 1 minute; transfer to wire racks to cool completely.

5 Dust cutout cookies with confectioners' sugar. Spread each solid cookie with about 1 teaspoon apricot preserves; top each with a cutout cookie. Store in an airtight container.

Don't toss those little pieces that you're cutting out of the cookies...they make perfect little nibblers!

Chocolate Nut Rugulach

Makes 32

⅓ cup plus ¼ cup sugar, divided

1 stick butter, softened

4 ounces cream cheese, softened

1 cup all-purpose flour

2 tablespoons unsweetened cocoa powder

¼ teaspoon salt

½ teaspoon vanilla extract

1 cup chocolate hazelnut filling (like Nutella), warmed for easier spreading

½ teaspoon cinnamon

½ cup chopped pecans

1 In a large bowl, cream ⅓ cup sugar, butter, and cream cheese. Mix in flour, cocoa, salt, and vanilla, stirring to make a soft dough. Add a little flour, as necessary, if dough is too sticky. Wrap in plastic and chill 1 hour or overnight.

2 Preheat oven to 350 degrees F. Line 2 baking sheets with parchment paper. Divide dough in half. Place half back in refrigerator until ready to use.

3 On a well-floured cutting board, roll dough into a 10-inch circle. Cut dough into 16 pie-shaped wedges. Spread chocolate hazelnut filling over dough. Repeat with remaining dough.

4 In a small bowl, combine remaining sugar and cinnamon; mix well. Sprinkle over filling. Top with pecans. Roll up each wedge starting from wide end and place on prepared baking sheets.

5 Bake 22 to 25 minutes, or until firm. Let cool, then store in an airtight container.

Serving Suggestion:
These look great with a light dusting of confectioners' sugar sprinkled on right before serving.

Notes

Frozen & Refrigerated Treats

Frozen Black & White Squares

Serves 9

1 (8-ounce) container frozen whipped topping, thawed, divided

½ cup hot fudge topping, slightly warmed

2 cups crushed chocolate sandwich cookies (about 16 cookies), divided

11 vanilla ice cream sandwiches

1 In a medium bowl, combine half the whipped topping and the hot fudge until well blended. Fold in 1 cup crushed cookies.

2 In an 8-inch-square baking dish, arrange ½ the ice cream sandwiches in a single layer, cutting one or two, if necessary, to fit dish. Cover with half the whipped topping mixture. Top with remaining ice cream sandwiches to form another single layer. Top with remaining whipped topping mixture. Sprinkle with remaining cookies.

3 Wrap loosely with foil and freeze 4 hours, or until ready to serve.

Individual Baked Alaskas

Makes 6

6 single-serving graham cracker tart shells

1 quart strawberry ice cream

⅓ cup strawberry preserves

2 egg whites

3 tablespoons sugar

⅛ teaspoon cream of tartar

1 Place the tart shells on a baking sheet. Place one scoop of ice cream into each; top each with about 1 tablespoon preserves. Place in freezer. When the ice cream tarts are completely frozen, preheat oven to broil.

2 In a small bowl with an electric mixer on medium speed, beat egg whites until foamy; continue beating while adding sugar and cream of tartar. Beat until stiff peaks form, making meringue.

3 Remove ice cream tarts from freezer and quickly spread meringue over ice cream, making sure to completely cover the ice cream and top edge of crust. Place back on baking sheet.

4 Broil 2 to 4 minutes, or until the meringue is golden. Remove from broiler and place on another baking sheet. Cover loosely and freeze at least 2 hours. When ready to serve, remove from freezer and allow to stand 5 minutes.

Did You Know?
The name "Baked Alaska" was coined at New York City's Delmonico's restaurant by their chef in 1867 to honor the recently acquired American territory of Alaska. (Just a fun fact to share while serving these up!)

Caramel Frozen Squares

Serves 10

1-½ cups packed light brown sugar

½ cup evaporated milk

7 tablespoons butter, melted, divided

½ teaspoon vanilla extract

1 (13-ounce) package pecan shortbread cookies

½ gallon vanilla ice cream, softened

1 In a small saucepan, over medium-low heat, combine brown sugar and evaporated milk; bring to a boil. Reduce heat to low and simmer 2 to 3 minutes, stirring constantly. Remove from heat and stir in 1 tablespoon butter and the vanilla; set caramel sauce aside to cool.

2 Place cookies in a resealable plastic bag, seal, and using a rolling pin, crush cookies to the consistency of medium-coarse crumbs; set aside 1-½ cups of crumbs.

3 In a medium bowl, combine remaining crumbs with remaining butter. Coat a 9- x 13-inch baking dish with cooking spray. Press crumb mixture into baking dish. Pour ¾ of the caramel sauce over crumb crust. Carefully cover with ice cream.

4 Evenly drizzle remaining sauce over ice cream. Top with reserved cookie crumbs. Cover and freeze at least 3 hours, or until firm.

Serving Suggestion:
These can be cut into squares and individually wrapped and frozen to enjoy one at a time if you're not expecting a big crowd.

Bavarian Ice Cream Cake

Serves 12

1 (19.6-ounce) frozen chocolate layer cake, cut into 14 even slices (Do not thaw)

1 quart black cherry ice cream, slightly softened

1 (16-ounce) jar hot fudge sauce, divided, with 2 tablespoons reserved for drizzling

1 (8-ounce) container frozen whipped topping, thawed

12 maraschino or fresh cherries, pitted

1. Place half the cake slices in an 8-inch-square baking dish, arranging to fit tightly. Spread ice cream evenly over cake. Spoon half the hot fudge sauce over ice cream and top with remaining cake slices. Spoon remaining hot fudge sauce (except the 2 tablespoons reserved) over cake, then top with whipped topping.

2. Cover with plastic wrap and freeze 3 to 4 hours, or overnight.

3. Remove from freezer 5 to 10 minutes before serving. Warm reserved hot fudge sauce, drizzle over cake, and garnish with cherries. Serve immediately.

Did You Know?
You can find frozen layer cakes in the freezer section of the market along with other frozen desserts.

Frozen Chocolate Chip Fantasy

Serves 10

½ cup milk

½ cup coffee-flavored liqueur

34 chocolate chip cookies,
    with 2 reserved for garnish

2 (8-ounce) containers frozen
    whipped topping, thawed,
    divided

1. Line a 9- x 5-inch loaf pan with plastic wrap, with ends extending over sides of pan.

2. In a medium bowl, combine milk and coffee liqueur; mix well. Dip 8 chocolate chip cookies quickly into milk mixture and place in bottom of pan. Spoon one-third of one container of whipped topping evenly over cookies. Repeat two more times and top with a final layer of cookies.

3. Cover with ends of plastic wrap and freeze overnight.

4. Remove from freezer and invert onto a serving platter, removing the plastic wrap. Frost the entire loaf with remaining container of whipped topping. Crush remaining 2 cookies and sprinkle over top. Slice and serve, or keep frozen until ready to serve.

Lighten It Up:
It's probably hard to imagine that anything this rich and decadent could be made lighter and still taste great. Well it can! Just use low fat milk, reduced fat cookies, and a lighter whipped topping.

Frozen Mudslide Bombe

Serves 10

1 (19.8-ounce) package brownie mix, prepared according to package directions for a 9- x 13-inch baking dish (see Tip)

1 quart coffee ice cream, softened

2 cups frozen whipped topping, thawed

½ cup hot fudge sauce

1 Allow prepared brownies to cool, then cut into squares.

2 Line a (2-½-quart) freezer-safe bowl with plastic wrap. Line the bowl with about ⅔ of the brownies; press brownies together, molding them to the bowl, up to about 1 inch from top of bowl.

3 Spoon ice cream into bowl and press firmly over brownie crust, completely covering it. Place remaining brownies over top and press firmly into ice cream. Cover with plastic wrap and freeze overnight.

4 Invert onto a serving platter. Remove bowl and plastic wrap, then frost with whipped topping. Return to freezer 1 hour, or until whipped topping is frozen. Drizzle with hot fudge sauce and serve immediately.

Test Kitchen Mr. Food Hints & Tips

Slightly underbaked, fudgy brownies are perfect for this recipe because they'll be easier to press into the bowl.

Crunchy Almond Ice Cream Balls

Serves 8

1 quart vanilla ice cream

2-½ cups oven-toasted corn cereal, coarsely crushed

1 tablespoon butter, melted

½ cup sliced almonds

½ teaspoon almond extract

2 tablespoons sugar

1 teaspoon ground cinnamon

1 Line a rimmed baking sheet with wax paper. With an ice cream scoop, form eight ice cream balls, each about 2-½ inches in diameter. Place on baking sheet, then place in the freezer about 1 hour to firm up.

2 Meanwhile, preheat oven to 350 degrees F. Coat another large rimmed baking sheet with cooking spray.

3 In a medium bowl, combine remaining ingredients; mix well and spread on prepared baking sheet. Bake 5 to 7 minutes, or until lightly browned and crisp. Remove to a shallow dish and allow to cool completely.

4 Line baking sheet with clean wax paper. Remove ice cream balls from freezer and roll in cereal mixture, coating on all sides. Place on prepared baking sheet and freeze 2 to 3 hours, or until ice cream is firm. Serve immediately, or cover and keep frozen until ready to serve.

Serving Suggestion:
When it's time to serve, bring out the honey or caramel sauce and drizzle a bit on each ball. It adds an extra layer of goodness to each serving.

Frozen Banana Pudding Loaf

Serves 12

- 3 large bananas, peeled and sliced
- 1 (12-ounce) container frozen whipped topping, thawed, divided
- 1 (4-serving-size) package instant vanilla pudding and pie filling, prepared according to package directions
- 2 cups crushed vanilla wafers
- ¾ stick butter, melted

1 Line a 9- x 5-inch loaf pan with plastic wrap, with ends extending over sides of pan.

2 Stir banana slices and 2 cups whipped topping into pudding. Spoon into prepared pan.

3 In a medium bowl, combine crushed cookies and butter; mix well. Sprinkle over pudding mixture and gently press down. Cover with ends of plastic wrap.

4 Freeze 8 hours, or until firm. Invert onto serving platter; remove pan and plastic wrap. Cover with remaining whipped topping, slice and serve.

Serving Suggestion:
Garnish this with slices of banana and vanilla wafers. By the way, if you dip the banana slices in lemon juice, they won't turn brown.

Surprise Coffee Cups

Serves 12

4 cups (1 quart) coffee ice cream

12 chocolate candy truffles

¼ cup chocolate syrup

1 Line 12 muffin cups with paper liners; place a scoop of ice cream in each cup. Press a candy truffle into the center of each cup of ice cream, completely covering the candy with ice cream. Drizzle chocolate syrup over top.

2 Cover and place in freezer at least 3 to 4 hours, or until firm. Serve frozen.

This is so easy, yet looks so fancy. The key is all in the truffles. We tested these with both Lindt and generic store brands and both worked great. After a holiday it's a good time to find these on sale, so pick up a few packs to keep on hand.

Raspberry Margarita Madness

Serves 9

- 1 cup finely crushed pretzels
- 1 tablespoon sugar
- 1 stick butter, melted
- 1 (8-ounce) package cream cheese, softened
- 1 (14-ounce) can sweetened condensed milk
- ⅓ cup lime juice
- 3 tablespoons seedless raspberry jam
- 2 cups frozen whipped topping, thawed
- 1 cup fresh raspberries

1 In a medium bowl, combine pretzels, sugar, and butter; mix well. Press pretzel mixture over bottom of an 8-inch baking dish to form a crust; chill.

2 In a large bowl, with an electric mixer on medium speed, beat cream cheese until fluffy. Stir in sweetened condensed milk, lime juice, and raspberry jam; mix well. Fold in whipped topping and raspberries until well combined.

3 Pour into prepared baking dish; cover, and refrigerate at least 8 hours, or until firm.

Test Kitchen. Mr. Food Hints & Tips

We used pretzels in the crust since the combo of the salt and the lime juice makes these that much more authentic-tasting.

Frozen Chocolate Coconut Mounds

Serves 6

6 chocolate wafer cookies

1 pint vanilla ice cream, slightly softened

1 cup shredded coconut

2 tablespoons chopped almonds

⅓ cup chocolate-flavored hard-shell topping

1 Line a 6-cup muffin tin with paper liners and place a cookie in each.

2 In a large bowl, combine ice cream and coconut; mix well. Place a rounded scoop of ice cream mixture into each cup. Top each with chopped almonds and freeze 1 hour, or until firm.

3 Drizzle each with hard-shell topping until tops are completely covered. Freeze until chocolate shell is firm. Serve, or cover and keep frozen until ready to serve.

Lighten It Up:

First of all, you may want to use reduced-fat wafer cookies, and then pick up some vanilla frozen yogurt instead of the ice cream. Remember every bit helps.

Cranberry-Studded Rice Pudding

Serves 8

8 cups (½ gallon) milk

1 cup uncooked long- or whole-grain rice

3 egg yolks, beaten

¾ cup sugar

½ cup dried cranberries

½ teaspoon vanilla extract

1 In a large pot, combine the milk, rice, egg yolks, and sugar. Bring to a boil over medium heat, and cook 20 to 25 minutes, or until thickened and the rice is tender, stirring frequently to keep the rice from sticking.

2 Remove from heat, stir in cranberries and vanilla, and allow to cool slightly.

3 Spoon into a serving bowl or individual dessert dishes, and chill 2 to 3 hours. Serve, or cover and keep chilled until ready to serve.

Good For You!

Who would imagine that a rich, old-fashioned favorite like this would be chock-full of so many good benefits? From calcium-rich milk, protein-packed eggs, and fiber-packed whole grain rice to heart-healthy cranberries, it all adds up to a whole lot of "OOH IT'S SO GOOD!!"

Potluck Orange Cream

Serves 10

2 (4-serving-size) packages orange-flavored gelatin

3 cups boiling water

1 quart orange sherbet

2 cups frozen whipped topping, thawed

1. Place gelatin in a large bowl and add boiling water; stir until gelatin is dissolved. Stir in sherbet until it melts into gelatin mixture. Fold whipped topping into sherbet mixture and pour into a 10-inch Bundt pan.

2. Refrigerate overnight to set. When ready to serve, unmold it from pan and cut into slices.

Serving Suggestion:
Make this really picture-perfect by garnishing with dollops of whipped topping and fresh orange slices.

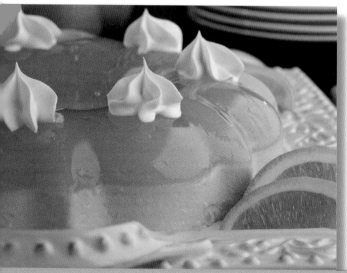

Pistachio Icebox Cake

Serves 12

2 (4-serving-size) packages instant pistachio pudding and pie filling, prepared according to package directions

1 (8-ounce) container frozen whipped topping, thawed

¼ cup plus 2 tablespoons coarsely chopped pistachios, divided

1 (14.4-ounce) package chocolate-flavored graham crackers

1 (16-ounce) container chocolate frosting

1 In a medium bowl, combine pudding mix, whipped topping, and ¼ cup chopped pistachios. Place a single layer of graham crackers in bottom of a 9- x 13-inch baking dish. Top with one-third of pudding mixture.

2 Repeat layers of graham crackers and pudding 2 more times, ending with a layer of graham crackers.

3 Spread frosting over top, sprinkle with remaining chopped pistachios, then cover and chill overnight, allowing graham crackers to soften. Cut into squares and serve.

Yes, this can be made in advance and kept frozen so you always have a little something on hand when friends stop by.

Mocha Marshmallow Mousse

Serves 6 or makes 12 mini servings

3 (1-ounce) squares semisweet
 chocolate

4 ounces cream cheese, softened

1 tablespoon instant coffee granules

2 tablespoons hot water

1 teaspoon vanilla extract

1 (7-ounce) jar marshmallow creme

1 (8-ounce) container frozen whipped
 topping, thawed

1 In a large microwaveable bowl, melt the chocolate on high power 1-½ to 2 minutes; stir until completely melted and smooth. Add cream cheese and mix with an electric mixer on medium speed, until well blended.

2 In a cup, dissolve coffee in hot water and add to cream cheese mixture. Add vanilla and beat until well combined. Blend in marshmallow creme, then fold in whipped topping. Cover and refrigerate at least 1 hour before serving.

Serving suggestion:

This can also be made and served easily in individual mini dessert dishes like we did here. Top each with a mini marshmallow and serve with a crisp cookie! (We think our Almond Florentine Cookies are the perfect match. See page 97 for the recipe.)

Mixed Berry Trifle

Serves 6

1 fresh or thawed frozen pound cake, cut into 1-inch cubes

1 cup raspberries, with a few reserved for garnish

1 cup blueberries, with a few reserved for garnish

1 cup blackberries, with a few reserved for garnish

1 (4-serving-size) package instant vanilla pudding and pie filling, prepared according to package directions

2 cups thawed frozen whipped topping (an 8-ounce container equals 3-½ cups)

1 Arrange half the cake cubes in a 2-quart glass serving bowl or trifle dish.

2 In a medium bowl, combine the berries. Spoon half the berries over cake; spread with half the pudding. Repeat with remaining cake cubes, berries, and pudding.

3 Cover and chill at least 4 hours. Spread whipped topping over trifle and garnish with remaining berries when ready to serve.

To give this an even more intense flavor, try tossing the berries with a couple of tablespoons of raspberry or orange liqueur before layering them.

Crème Caramel

Serves 8

¾ cup sugar, divided

4 eggs

1 teaspoon vanilla extract

2 cups milk

1 Preheat oven to 350 degree F.

2 In a small nonstick skillet over medium heat, stir ½ cup sugar until completely melted and caramel-colored, about 6 minutes. Immediately pour caramelized sugar into a 9-inch glass pie plate, coating bottom of plate. (Be careful when working with heated sugar; it is very hot.)

3 In a medium bowl, beat eggs with vanilla. In a small bowl, combine milk with remaining sugar, then beat into egg mixture. Pour over caramelized sugar then place pie plate into a roasting pan with just enough hot water to go about halfway up sides of pie plate.

4 Bake 40 minutes, or until a knife inserted in center comes out clean. Let cool 20 minutes then cover and chill 1 hour, or until ready to serve. Right before serving, invert custard onto a 10- or 12-inch rimmed serving plate so caramel sauce doesn't run off plate.

Easy Tiramisu

Serves 8

1 (16-ounce) package mascarpone cheese

1-¼ cups heavy cream

¼ cup confectioners' sugar

1-½ teaspoons vanilla extract

1 cup strong black coffee

2 tablespoons rum

2 (3-ounce) packages ladyfingers

4 (1-ounce) bittersweet chocolate squares, grated

1 In a large bowl with an electric mixer on high speed, beat mascarpone cheese, heavy cream, confectioners' sugar, and vanilla 30 seconds, or just until blended.

2 In a small bowl, stir together coffee and rum .

3 Arrange 1 package ladyfingers in bottom of a 3-quart bowl or trifle dish; brush with half coffee mixture. Layer half mascarpone cheese mixture over ladyfingers; sprinkle with half grated chocolate. Repeat layers. Cover and chill 8 hours.

Did You Know?

Tasting is just one of the perks of being in the Test Kitchen. Maybe that's why Patty and Kelly love their jobs so much!

Cobblers, Crumbles, Crisps & More

Cobbler in a Skillet

Serves 8

2 (21-ounce) cans pie filling
  (see Tip)

¼ cup sugar

½ teaspoon ground cinnamon

1 (10.2-ounce) package refrigerated
  buttermilk biscuits (5 biscuits),
  each biscuit cut into 6 pieces

¼ stick butter, melted

1 Preheat oven to 375 degrees F.

2 In a cast iron skillet, heat the pie filling over medium heat until hot.

3 Meanwhile, in a large bowl, combine sugar, cinnamon, biscuit pieces, and butter; mix until evenly coated. Place mixture over pie filling.

4 Place skillet in oven and bake 15 to 20 minutes, or until golden.

Test Kitchen. Mr. Food Hints & Tips

Feel free to use your favorite type of pie filling, or even try mixing-n-matching flavors. Just look how yummy it looks when we used strawberry pie filling and even mixed in a few fresh berries that we cut up.

Plum Good Crumble

Serves 8

8 fresh plums, pitted and thinly sliced

½ cup water

½ cup plus ⅓ cup sugar, divided

¼ cup cornstarch

¼ teaspoon salt

½ cup all-purpose flour

½ teaspoon ground cinnamon

¼ teaspoon ground nutmeg

½ stick butter

1 Preheat oven to 350 degrees F.

2 In a large saucepan, combine plums and water; cover, bring to a boil, and cook 5 minutes. Reduce heat to medium and add ½ cup sugar, cornstarch, and salt and cook 3 to 4 minutes, or until thickened, stirring occasionally. Pour into an 8-inch-square baking dish.

3 In a medium bowl, mix together remaining sugar, flour, cinnamon, nutmeg, and butter; sprinkle evenly over the plums.

4 Bake 35 to 40 minutes, or until crumbs are golden and plum filling is bubbly.

No plums? No worries! Simply substitute nectarines or peaches for equally delicious fresh crumble. And oh, don't forget to pick up some vanilla ice cream at the market. It's the perfect accent to this bubblin' hot dessert.

Sun-Kissed Blueberry Crisp

Serves 8

1 (21-ounce) can blueberry pie filling

1 cup fresh blueberries

1 tablespoon lemon zest

½ cup quick-cooking oats

3 tablespoons light brown sugar

¼ cup all-purpose flour

¼ stick butter

1. Preheat oven to 400 degrees F. Coat an 8-inch-square baking dish with cooking spray.

2. In a large bowl, combine blueberry pie filling, blueberries, and lemon zest; mix well. Spoon into prepared baking dish; set aside.

3. In a medium bowl, combine oats, brown sugar, and flour; mix well. With a fork, blend in butter until crumbly; sprinkle over blueberries.

4. Bake 30 to 35 minutes, or until golden and bubbly. Serve warm.

Serving Suggestion:
Wanna make individual portions? Dig out those ramekins or small crocks. Fill them about ¾ full with the blueberry mixture, finish them off with the topping, place them on a baking sheet, and bake. Just be aware the baking time will be shorter since they're smaller.

French Strawberry-Rhubarb Bake

Serves 8

1 quart fresh strawberries, washed, hulled, and sliced

2 cups frozen rhubarb, thawed

⅓ cup sugar

1 tablespoon cornstarch

½ loaf French bread, cut into ½-inch cubes (about 4 cups)

1 stick butter, melted

1 Preheat oven to 375 degrees F. Coat a 2-quart casserole dish with cooking spray.

2 In a large bowl, combine strawberries, rhubarb, sugar, and cornstarch; toss to coat. Add bread cubes and melted butter; mix well. Spoon into prepared casserole dish.

3 Bake 30 to 35 minutes, or until bread is golden. Serve warm.

Test Kitchen. Mr. Food. Hints & Tips

When life gives you fresh rhubarb...take advantage of it! Trim off the leaves and simply cut it up into 1-inch pieces. Place it in a pan with enough water to cover it and boil until it's tender. Then drain it, cool it and measure what you need and you can freeze the rest.

Chocolate Pecan Cobbler

Serves 8

¾ stick butter

1-¾ cups sugar, divided

1 cup all-purpose flour

½ teaspoon salt

1-½ teaspoons baking powder

6 tablespoons unsweetened cocoa powder, divided

½ cup milk

1 teaspoon vanilla extract

½ cup chopped pecans

½ cup toffee bits

1-½ cups boiling water

1. Preheat oven to 350 degrees F. In a shallow 3-quart casserole dish or 9-inch deep dish pie plate, melt butter in microwave, about 1 minute; set aside.

2. In a medium bowl, combine ¾ cup sugar, the flour, salt, baking powder, and 2 tablespoons cocoa. Add milk and vanilla, whisking until smooth. Pour over melted butter.

3. In another medium bowl, combine remaining sugar, remaining cocoa, the pecans, and toffee bits; sprinkle over sugar mixture. Slowly pour boiling water over the top.

4. Bake 35 to 40 minutes, or until cobbler is set. Serve piping hot.

Serving Suggestion:

For extreme decadence, we suggest topping this with freshly made whipped cream (see our recipe on page 159) and more chopped pecans. Yummy!

Apple Pan Betty

Serves 4

½ stick butter

2 large tart apples, peeled and cubed

2 cups French bread cubes (see Tip)

¼ cup sugar

½ teaspoon ground cinnamon

1 In a skillet over medium heat, melt butter. Stir in apples and sauté 4 to 5 minutes, or until tender. Stir in bread cubes, sugar, and cinnamon. Cook 5 to 7 minutes, or until bread is warmed. Serve immediately.

To make this as authentic as possible, cut a French or Italian bread from the bakery into 1-inch cubes. The best part is, you won't even need a full loaf, so make sure you have some butter on hand to slather on the leftover bread as a snack while the pan betty cooks.

Good Ol' Raspberry Cobbler

Serves 8

2 (21-ounce) cans raspberry
pie filling

1 (11-ounce) can mandarin
oranges, drained

1 cup biscuit baking mix

½ cup milk

1 egg

1 Preheat oven to 400 degrees F. Coat a 3-quart casserole dish with cooking spray.

2 In a large bowl, combine raspberry pie filling and mandarin oranges; mix well. Pour into prepared casserole dish; set aside.

3 In a medium bowl, whisk remaining ingredients until well blended. Pour over raspberry mixture.

4 Bake uncovered 30 to 35 minutes, or until crust is golden.

Did You Know?

Biscuit baking mix is a great shortcut when baking or making pancakes since it contains flour, sugar, salt, vegetable shortening, and baking soda. That means less ingredients to store and less to clean up.

Extreme Caramel Apple Crisp

Serves 8

2 (20-ounce) cans sliced apples in water, drained (not apple pie filling)

½ cup plus 3 tablespoons sugar, divided

2 tablespoons cornstarch

½ teaspoon ground cinnamon

20 caramel candies, unwrapped

1 cup all-purpose flour

¼ teaspoon salt

½ stick butter, softened

3 tablespoons heavy cream

½ cup semisweet chocolate chips

1. Preheat oven to 400 degrees F. Coat an 8-inch-square baking dish with cooking spray.

2. In a large bowl, combine apples, ½ cup sugar, the cornstarch, cinnamon, and caramels; mix well then pour into prepared baking dish.

3. In a medium bowl, combine flour, remaining sugar, the salt, butter, and cream; mix until crumbly. Sprinkle over apple mixture.

4. Bake 30 to 35 minutes, or until bubbly and top is golden.

5. In a microwaveable bowl, melt chocolate chips in the microwave 30 to 60 seconds, or until melted, stirring occasionally. (Do not overcook!) Cool slightly, then place in a plastic storage bag; snip a pencil tip-sized hole in the corner of the bag and drizzle over crumb topping, let cool slightly.

If you prefer to use fresh apples, simply peel, core and slice about 3 pounds and you should be good to go. Another option would be to use 2 (16-ounce) bags frozen sliced apples.

Pineapple Cherry Crumble

Serves 9

- 1 (20-ounce) can pineapple chunks, drained
- 1 (20-ounce) can cherry pie filling
- 1 (18.25-ounce) package yellow cake mix
- 1 stick butter, sliced into pats

1 Preheat oven to 350 degrees F. Coat a 9- x 13-inch baking dish with cooking spray.

2 Place pineapple chunks in bottom of prepared baking dish. Spoon cherry pie filling over top and sprinkle with dry cake mix. Top with butter pats.

3 Bake 30 to 35 minutes, or until golden. Allow to cool slightly; serve warm.

Serving Suggestion:
Ready to really wow them? Top a big scoop of vanilla ice cream with a generous helping of the crumble for an old-fashioned-tasting twist on an ice cream sundae. Just thinking about this makes our mouths water!

Cinnamon Pear Crisp

Serves 8

4 (15-ounce) cans sliced pears, drained

½ cup plus 3 tablespoons sugar, divided

2 tablespoons cornstarch

½ teaspoon ground cinnamon

2 tablespoons cinnamon candies (like Red Hots)

1 cup all-purpose flour

¼ teaspoon salt

½ stick butter, softened

3 tablespoons heavy cream

1. Preheat oven to 400 degrees F. Coat an 8-inch-square baking dish with cooking spray.

2. In a large bowl, combine pears, ½ cup sugar, cornstarch, cinnamon, and cinnamon candies; mix well then pour into prepared baking dish.

3. In a medium bowl, combine flour, remaining sugar, salt, butter, and cream; mix until crumbly. Sprinkle over pear mixture.

4. Bake 30 to 35 minutes, or until bubbly and top is golden.

Test Kitchen. Mr. Food Hints & Tips

We really like the spicy kick that the cinnamon candies add to this crisp. And with the leftover candies, try melting a teaspoon or so in a cup of hot tea for a rich cinnamon accent.

Peachy Graham Cracker Crumble

Serves 8

6 peaches, pitted and thinly sliced

¾ cup packed light brown sugar

1 cup coarsely crushed graham crackers

¼ teaspoon cinnamon

3 tablespoons butter, melted

1. Preheat oven to 375 degrees F. Coat an 8-inch-square baking dish with cooking spray. Combine peaches and brown sugar in baking dish.

2. In a small bowl, combine graham cracker crumbs, cinnamon, and butter. Sprinkle graham cracker topping over peaches.

3. Bake 30 to 35 minutes, or until peaches are hot and bubbly. Serve warm.

Serving Suggeston:

Go peach-crazy by serving this up with some peach ice cream. We suggest putting the ice cream in the bottom of the bowl rather than on the top.

Fresh Whipped Cream

Makes about 2 cups

1 cup heavy cream

1 tablespoon confectioners' sugar

½ teaspoon vanilla extract

1 In a medium bowl with an electric mixer on high speed, whip cream and sugar 3 to 5 minutes, or until soft peaks form. Add vanilla and whip until stiff peaks form (and hold together like whipped cream is supposed to).

To make ready-to-use whipped cream dollops: Spoon heaping teaspoon-sized dollops of whipped cream onto a wax paper-lined baking sheet. Freeze 1-½ hours, or until solid. Transfer dollops to a plastic bag, close tightly, and store in freezer until ready to use. Just before serving, remove desired number of dollops and allow to thaw before using. (These thaw in minutes and will last in the freezer up to 1 month.)

Add a teaspoon of cinnamon right before whipping the cream and sugar to add just the right touch for all your fall fruit dishes.

COBBLERS, CRISPS, CRUMBLES...
what's the difference?

Ok, we admit it. We too were a bit confused by the differences between all these fruit-filled desserts that fill our kitchen with a heavenly scent.

So after a bit of researching and testing lots of recipes, we think we figured out what is what. Now it's time for us to share our findings with you.

Cobbler – One of the most popular of all the warm fruit desserts is a cobbler! A lot like a pot pie, this bubblin' hot deep-dish fruit bake boasting a thick, golden flaky biscuit-style crust atop a fresh or frozen sliced fruit or berry filling always shouts comfort.

Crisp – What sets a warm fruit-filled crisp apart from the rest is that the sweetened fruit filling is covered with a crumbly topping made from flour, sugar, butter, spices and sometimes other ingredients like rolled oats and nuts.

Crumble – A crumble is actually the British version of the all-American crisp! It's also made with a "crumbly" streusel-style topping that's thrown together with flour, sugar, butter, spices and chopped nuts.

Buckle – This melt-in-your-mouth warm coffee cake-like dessert is dotted with fruit or berries and sprinkled with a crumble-style streusel topping!

Slump – No baking required for this one, 'cause a slump cooks right on your stovetop! It's chock full of sweetened fruit that's topped with generous dollops of dough and often served with heavy cream.

Grunt – This old fashioned one is another "keep the kitchen cool" dumpling-like fruit-filled dessert. It's made by placing the baking dish in a container of simmering water to steam it to tasty perfection.

Betty – With its crispy golden brown top, this baked pudding made from alternating layers of sugar 'n' spiced fruit, buttered bread crumbs and a bit of fruit juice to moisten it; was very popular in colonial America.

Pandowdy – Right in the midst of baking this deep dish fruit pie that's sweetened with molasses or brown sugar and topped with a biscuit-like dough, the crust is broken up ("dowdying") and pressed down into the fruit so it can absorb the juices.

This & That

Crème-Filled Eclairs

Serves 10

1 cup water

1 stick butter

¼ teaspoon salt

1 cup all-purpose flour

4 eggs, at room temperature

1 (12-ounce) container frozen whipped topping, thawed

1 (16-ounce) container chocolate frosting

For an extra-special touch, try using a double batch of our Fresh Whipped Cream (see recipe on page 159) instead of the whipped topping.

1 Preheat oven to 400 degrees F. In a medium saucepan over medium-high heat, bring water, butter, and salt to a boil. Add flour all at once and stir quickly with a wooden spoon until mixture forms a ball; remove from heat.

2 Add 1 egg to mixture and beat hard with wooden spoon to blend. Add remaining eggs one at a time, beating well after each addition; each egg must be completely blended before the next egg is added. While beating dough, its consistency will change from looking almost curdled to smooth. When dough is smooth, spoon it into a large resealable plastic storage bag and, using scissors, snip off one corner of bag, making a 1-inch-wide cut. Gently squeeze bag to form ten 1- x 4-inch dough logs about 2 inches apart on an ungreased large rimmed baking sheet.

3 Bake 30 to 35 minutes, or until golden and puffy. Remove to a wire rack to cool.

4 Cut eclair shells horizontally in half and spread whipped topping equally into bottom of each. Replace tops of eclair shells.

5 Meanwhile, place frosting in a microwaveable bowl. Microwave, stopping to stir frequently, until it has the texture of lightly whipped cream, about 30 to 45 seconds. Pour melted frosting over éclairs. Cover loosely and chill at least 1 hour before serving.

Strawberry Shortcake Trifle

Serves 10

1 (16.3-ounce) package refrigerated buttermilk biscuits (8 biscuits)

1 (4-serving-size) package instant vanilla pudding and pie filling

1-½ cups milk

1 (8-ounce) container frozen whipped topping, thawed, divided

1 quart fresh strawberries

1 Place biscuits on a baking sheet and bake according to package directions. Remove from oven and let cool.

2 Meanwhile, in a large bowl, whisk pudding mix and milk together until thickened. Stir in half the whipped topping until combined.

3 Wash strawberries; hull, and slice all but 3, keeping those reserved for garnish.

4 Break cooled biscuits into large pieces and place half of them in the bottom of a large glass bowl or trifle dish. Spoon half the pudding mixture over that and layer with half the strawberries. Repeat layers and top with remaining whipped topping. Garnish with reserved whole strawberries.

Raspberry Peach Tart

Serves 8

- 1 rolled refrigerated pie crust (from a 15-ounce package)
- ½ cup fresh raspberries OR frozen raspberries, thawed
- 3 cups fresh peeled and sliced peaches OR frozen peeled and sliced peaches, thawed
- 3 tablespoons sugar, divided
- 1 tablespoon apple jelly, melted

1 Preheat oven to 425 degrees F. Place pie crust on a rimmed baking sheet.

2 In a large bowl, combine raspberries, peaches, and 2 tablespoons sugar. Arrange mixture in center of dough, leaving a 2-inch border.

3 Fold edges of dough toward center, (see photo below) pressing gently to seal (dough will only partially cover peach mixture). Brush melted jelly over peach mixture and edges of dough.

4 Bake 10 minutes, then reduce oven temperature to 350 degrees F. Bake 20 additional minutes, or until lightly browned.

5 Sprinkle with remaining sugar. Serve warm or at room temperature.

Butterscotch Cheese Ball

Makes 1 (4-inch) ball

---

2 (8-ounce) packages cream cheese, softened

½ stick butter, softened

¼ cup brown sugar

1 cup confectioners' sugar

1 teaspoon vanilla extract

1 teaspoon imitation butter extract

1 cup butterscotch chips

1 cup chopped pecans

½ cup butterscotch ice cream topping

1 In a large bowl, with an electric mixer, mix cream cheese and butter. Add brown sugar and confectioners' sugar, vanilla, and butter extract. Fold in chips. Cover and chill 1 hour, or until firm.

2 Form into a ball, roll in chopped pecans, and place on a serving platter. Refrigerate 3 hours, or until ready to serve.

3 Before serving, drizzle with butterscotch ice cream topping.

Serving Suggestion:
Just like with a traditional cheese ball, you need go-alongs, so try pear and apple slices, vanilla wafers, or pretzels.

Shortcut Chocolate-Glazed Donuts

Serves 10

- 1 cup confectioners' sugar
- 1 tablespoon unsweetened cocoa powder
- 2 tablespoons water
- 1 (7.5-ounce) package refrigerated biscuits (10 biscuits)
- Vegetable oil for cooking

1 In a medium bowl, combine confectioners' sugar, cocoa, and water; mix well to make glaze and set aside. Separate biscuits and lay flat on a cutting board. Using an apple corer or a sharp knife, cut out a small circle in the center of each biscuit, forming doughnut shapes.

2 In a soup pot over high heat, heat 1 inch of oil until hot but not smoking.

3 Cook doughnuts in batches about 1 minute per side, or until golden. Drain on a paper towel-lined baking sheet.

4 While still hot, dip doughnuts in glaze, turning to coat completely. Place on a wire rack that has been placed over a baking sheet, to allow excess glaze to drip off. Serve warm.

Test Kitchen, Mr. Food Hints & Tips

No sense wasting those small pieces of dough you cut from the center of the doughnut. Fry them up too!

Homemade Peanut Butter Cups

Makes 12

2 cups milk chocolate chips, divided

3 tablespoons vegetable shortening, divided

1-½ cups confectioners' sugar

1 cup creamy peanut butter

½ stick butter, softened

1 Line a 12-cup muffin tin with paper liners.

2 In a small saucepan over low heat, melt 1-¼ cups chocolate chips and 2 tablespoons shortening, stirring just until mixture is smooth. Allow to cool slightly; mixture should still be pourable.

3 Starting halfway up each paper liner, spoon about 2 teaspoons mixture over inside of cups, completely covering bottom half of each cup. Chill cups about 30 minutes, or until firm.

4 In a large bowl, combine confectioners' sugar, peanut butter, and butter; mix well. (Mixture will be dry.) Spoon evenly into chocolate cups and press down firmly.

5 Place remaining chocolate chips and shortening in saucepan and melt over low heat, stirring just until mixture is smooth. Spoon equal amounts into cups, spreading to completely cover peanut butter mixture. Cover and chill at least 2 hours, or until firm.

Lemon Whoopie Pies

Makes 15

1 (18.25-ounce) package lemon cake mix

⅓ cup water

½ cup vegetable oil

3 eggs

1 (8-ounce) package cream cheese, softened

1 stick butter, softened

1 teaspoon vanilla extract

1 tablespoon lemon zest

4 cups confectioners' sugar

1 Preheat oven to 350 degrees F. Coat baking sheets with cooking spray.

2 In a large bowl, combine cake mix, water, oil, and eggs; beat well. Drop by tablespoonfuls onto prepared baking sheets, at least 3-inches apart.

3 Bake 7 to 8 minutes, or until a wooden toothpick inserted in center comes out clean. Let cool slightly, then remove to a wire rack to cool completely.

4 In a large bowl, beat cream cheese, butter, vanilla, and lemon zest until fluffy. Beat in confectioners' sugar, 1 cup at a time until smooth.

5 Turn half the cooled cakes over onto their rounded sides and spread a dollop of filling over them. Place the other half of the cakes on top of the filling, forming sandwiches. Refrigerate until ready to serve.

Fudgie Mini Soufflés

Makes 12

3 eggs, separated

2 cups semisweet chocolate chips

1 stick butter

¼ cup plus 1 teaspoon sugar, divided

¼ cup water

½ cup heavy cream

½ teaspoon vanilla extract

1 Preheat oven to 425 degrees F. Line a 12-cup muffin tin with paper liners.

2 In a medium bowl, beat egg whites until stiff peaks form; set aside.

3 In a medium saucepan, combine chocolate chips, butter, ¼ cup sugar, and the water over medium heat. Cook 2 to 3 minutes, or until the chocolate and butter have melted, stirring constantly. Remove from heat and quickly whisk in the egg yolks. Add beaten egg whites; fold until well combined. Pour evenly into baking cups.

4 Bake 8 to 10 minutes, or until puffed and the tops are dry.

5 Meanwhile, in a medium bowl, beat heavy cream, remaining sugar, and vanilla, until slightly thickened. Serve warm soufflés with the vanilla cream sauce.

Test Kitchen.
Mr. Food
Hints & Tips

To learn the most amazing way to separate an egg, go to mrfood.com and search "How to Separate Eggs". We promise it'll wow you!

White Chocolate Raspberry Bundles

Makes 4

1 sheet frozen puff pastry, (from a 17.25-ounce box) thawed for 30 minutes

¼ cup raspberry preserves

1 cup white chocolate chips

¼ cup chopped walnuts

Confectioners' sugar for sprinkling

1 Preheat oven to 425 degrees F.

2 On a lightly floured surface, roll pastry out to a 12-inch square; cut square into four 6-inch squares. Place 1 tablespoon raspberry preserves, ¼ cup white chocolate chips, and 1 tablespoon chopped walnuts in center of each square. Bring pastry corners together and gently twist the dough to seal; fan out the corners. Place on an ungreased baking sheet.

3 Bake 10 to 15 minutes, or until golden brown. Let stand 10 minutes, then sprinkle with confectioners' sugar and serve.

Lighten It Up:

We have tested this with sugar-free preserves and omitted the chocolate chips and it worked out just fine. So, if you or someone in your gang would prefer this option, go ahead and try it. There are no rules!

Pumpkin Spice Roll

Serves 8

¾ cup all-purpose flour

1 cup granulated sugar

1 teaspoon baking soda

2 teaspoons pumpkin pie spice

1 cup pumpkin puree

3 eggs

1 cup plus 2 tablespoons confectioners' sugar, divided

1 (8-ounce) package cream cheese, softened

½ stick butter

1 teaspoon vanilla extract

1 Preheat oven to 375 degrees F. Coat a rimmed 10- x 15-inch baking sheet with cooking spray.

2 In a large bowl, combine flour, granulated sugar, baking soda, and pumpkin pie spice. Stir in pumpkin and eggs. Pour mixture into prepared pan, spreading evenly.

3 Bake 12 to 15 minutes, or until a wooden toothpick inserted in center comes out clean. Remove from oven and invert onto a clean kitchen towel that has been sprinkled with 2 tablespoons confectioners' sugar. While cake is still hot, roll it up in towel jelly-roll style from the narrow end; cool on a wire rack. When cool, unroll cake and remove towel.

4 In a small bowl with an electric mixer on medium speed, beat cream cheese, butter, vanilla, and remaining confectioners' sugar. Spread onto cooled cake and immediately re-roll (without towel). Place on serving platter and refrigerate until ready to serve. Cut into slices just before serving.

To fancy this up a bit, right before serving, sprinkle on some confectioners' sugar. Ooh la la!

Cashew Caramel Bread Pudding

Serves 6

1 (1-pound) loaf day-old French or Italian bread, torn into 1-inch pieces

2 cups warm water

3 eggs

1 cup (½ pint) heavy cream

30 caramels, chopped

½ cup sugar

¾ cup cashews, coarsely chopped

1 teaspoon vanilla extract

1 teaspoon salt

1 Preheat oven to 350 degrees F. Coat a 2-quart casserole dish with cooking spray.

2 In a large bowl, toss together bread and water, soaking the bread.

3 In a small bowl, whisk eggs and stir in heavy cream. Add to bread, along with remaining ingredients. Place in prepared casserole dish

4 Bake 60 to 65 minutes, or until center is firm. Serve warm, or allow to cool completely, cover, and chill until ready to serve.

Serving Suggestion:

Want to go all out? Drizzle some lightly whipped heavy cream over each serving. It cuts the sweetness and adds a touch of creaminess...WOW!

Apple Pie Bites

Serves 16

½ cup sugar

2 teaspoons cinnamon

1 (8-ounce) can refrigerated crescent rolls

2 tablespoons butter, melted, divided

2 apples, peeled and cut into about 16 slices

1 Preheat oven to 425 degrees F. Line a baking sheet with parchment paper and coat with cooking spray. In a small bowl, combine sugar and cinnamon; set aside.

2 Unroll crescent dough, separating into 4 rectangles; press perforations to seal. Brush 1 tablespoon of butter evenly over dough, then sprinkle with about ½ of cinnamon sugar. Cut each rectangle into 4 strips.

3 Wrap each strip around an apple slice. Place on prepared baking sheet. Brush with remaining butter and sprinkle with remaining cinnamon sugar.

4 Bake 10 to 13 minutes, or until golden.

Test Kitchen. Mr. Food Hints & Tips

If you want to cut your apples in advance, soak them in some water and lemon juice to prevent them from browning. Before rolling them in the dough, make sure you dry them off well.

Peanut Butter Cup Parfaits

Serves 4

1 (4-serving-size) package instant vanilla pudding and pie filling

1-½ cups milk

½ cup peanut butter

1-½ cups frozen whipped topping, thawed, divided

4 tablespoons graham cracker crumbs, divided

1 cup coarsely chopped peanut butter cups

1 In a large bowl, using a wire whisk, combine pudding mix and milk until thickened. Whisk in peanut butter and 1 cup whipped topping.

2 Sprinkle 1 tablespoon crumbs into each of four parfait (or other tall) glasses. Divide half the peanut butter pudding mixture evenly into glasses. Sprinkle with half the peanut butter cups.

3 Repeat with remaining crumbs and peanut butter pudding mixture. Top each parfait with whipped topping and remaining peanut butter cups. Refrigerate until ready to serve.

Lighten It Up:
Ok, this will never be a "skinny mini" dessert, but by using reduced-fat peanut butter and lite whipped topping we can save lots of calories. Also, by simply cutting the portion size in half, you can save 50% of the calories.

Peach Foster Crepes

Makes 10

1 (1.5-quart) container French vanilla ice cream (see Tips)

10 (9-inch) ready-to-use crepes (from a 5-ounce package)

¾ stick butter

¾ cup light brown sugar

2 (15-ounce) cans sliced peaches, drained

1-½ cups frozen whipped topping, thawed

1 Using scissors, cut ice cream container several times so you can easily remove entire block of ice cream from container. Place on a cutting board and cut in half lengthwise. Cut each half lengthwise into 5 "logs." Place an ice cream log in center of each crepe and roll up. Place filled crepes, seam-side down, on a baking sheet and freeze until ready to serve.

2 Just before serving, in a medium skillet over medium heat, melt butter and add brown sugar. Cook for I minute, stirring occasionally. Add peaches and cook 4 to 5 minutes, or until heated through, stirring occasionally.

3 To serve, spoon warmed peaches over crepes and top with a dollop of whipped topping.

To make this easy, buy ice cream that comes in a block-style container, or you can place a couple of scoops in each crepe, spreading them together before rolling up. And as for the crepes, you can usually find them in the produce section of your market.

Pear Strudel

Serves 6

1 sheet frozen puff pastry,
(from a 17.25-ounce package)
thawed

⅓ cup sugar

2 teaspoons ground cinnamon

2 (15-ounce) cans sliced pears,
drained

⅓ cup raisins

¼ cup chopped walnuts

1 egg, beaten

1 Preheat oven to 400 degrees F. Place pastry on a baking sheet and unfold.

2 In a medium bowl, combine sugar and cinnamon; mix well; Reserve 2 teaspoons mixture. Add pears, raisins, and walnuts to remaining mixture; mix well.

3 Spoon mixture down center of dough. Cut slits in dough, 1 inch apart, down both sides of filling. Brush each dough strip with beaten egg and fold over dough. Brush top of pastry with remaining egg and sprinkle with reserved sugar mixture.

4 Bake 25 to 30 minutes, or until golden. Serve warm, or allow to cool before serving.

Salted Chocolate Pretzel Toffee

Makes 1-1/2 pounds

- 3 cups thin pretzels, broken into pieces
- 2 sticks butter
- 1 cup light brown sugar
- 2 cups semisweet chocolate chips
- 1 tablespoon sea salt

1 Preheat oven to 375 degrees F. Line a rimmed 10- x 15-inch baking sheet with parchment paper; set aside. Spread broken pretzels in pan.

2 In a small saucepan over medium heat, combine butter and brown sugar and bring to a boil. Cook 3 minutes without stirring. Carefully pour over pretzels. (Mixture will be very hot.)

3 Bake 5 minutes, then place pan on cooling rack and sprinkle chocolate chips evenly over top. When chocolate is melted, after about 2 minutes, spread evenly over toffee. Sprinkle with sea salt.

4 Let cool 2 to 3 hours, or until hard. Break into pieces.

Test Kitchen
Mr. Food
Hints & Tips

We found it best to store these at room temperature. (Just know that if your kitchen is warm, you may have to lick the chocolate off your fingers!) Just don't keep these in the fridge because the sugar in the toffee will crystallize.

Candy Bar Brownie Trifle

Serves 24

1 (19.8-ounce) package brownie mix

1 (6-serving-size) package instant vanilla pudding and pie filling

3 cups milk

¾ cup creamy peanut butter

3-½ cups coarsely chopped assorted candy bars, with ½ cup reserved for garnish

1 (16-ounce) container frozen whipped topping, thawed

1 Prepare brownies according to package directions for a 9- x 13-inch baking dish; allow to cool completely.

2 In a large bowl, whisk pudding mix and milk until slightly thickened. Whisk in peanut butter until thoroughly combined. Refrigerate 10 minutes.

3 Break up brownies into 1-inch pieces and place half in bottom of a trifle bowl or large glass serving bowl. Cover with half the pudding mixture, half the candy, and half the whipped topping. Repeat layers and garnish with reserved candy.

4 Cover and chill at least 2 hours before serving.

Trifle bowls are great for a crowd, but if you want to serve up individual portions, feel free to make these in wine or martini glasses.

To-Die-For Dessert Dip

Makes 4 cups

2 (8-ounce) packages cream cheese, softened

⅓ cup brown sugar

1 (8-ounce) package frozen whipped topping, thawed

2 cups chopped candy bars of your choice (we used Snickers)

1 In a bowl with an electric mixer on medium speed, mix together cream cheese and brown sugar. Fold in whipped topping and chopped candy bars. Spoon into a 9-inch pie plate.

2 Chill at least 1 hour.

Serving Suggestion:
Wondering what to dunk into this sweet, creamy dip? How about pretzels, apple slices, or graham crackers? We think those are the perfect dippers!

Potato Crunch Fudge

Makes 3 dozen pieces

2 (14-ounce) cans sweetened
 condensed milk

4 cups semisweet chocolate chips

3 cups potato sticks

1 In a large saucepan over medium heat, bring sweetened condensed milk to a rolling boil, stirring constantly. Remove from heat and add chocolate chips, stirring until smooth. Add potato sticks; mix well.

2 Spread into an 8-inch square baking dish and chill 3 to 4 hours, or until firm. Cut into squares and serve.

Did You Know?
Potato sticks were first made when a chef tried frying shoestring potatoes, in a similar fashion to French fries. The rest is history.

Frozen Hot Chocolate

Serves 4

⅓ cup sugar

⅓ cup unsweetened cocoa powder

6 ounces bittersweet chocolate, chopped, plus extra for garnish

1-½ cups cold milk, divided

4 cups ice

Whipped cream or topping for garnish

1 In a small saucepan over medium heat, mix sugar, cocoa, chocolate, and ½ cup milk until well combined and chocolate is melted, stirring occasionally. Remove from heat; stir in remaining milk.

2 Pour into blender with ice; blend until smooth. Serve immediately topped with whipped topping and garnished with additional chopped chocolate.

Did You Know:

Serendipity 3, a restaurant in New York City, is well known for their Frrrozen Hot Chocolate. *Although there are several different versions...we think ours is pretty darn tasty.*

Index

Index